The Dark Messiah
Magick, Gnosis and Religion

Brian J Allan

London, England
www.HealingsOfAtlantis.com

Healings Of Atlantis Ltd

Devon

England

UK

www.healingsofatlantis.com

Published in Great Britain, 2010

by 11th Dimension Publishing

ISBN 978-1-907126-09-3

A catalogue record for this book is available from the British Library.

Acknowledgements

I would like to thank Phil Gardiner for supplying the artwork for the cover and encouragement for information that the book contains.

My thanks go to Bill Downie for his invaluable advice on how the ancient technique of Gematria functions. My dear wife Ann, also deserves special mention for proof reading the original manuscript and of course, for her usual and much appreciated encouragement.

Finally, I would like to express my appreciation and gratitude to those who contribute to, monitor and facilitate the marvellous resource that is Wikipedia: I would gladly endorse and recommend this facility to anyone.

Contents

Introduction

The reader should be aware that this book concerns the nature of phenomena and practices associated with mysticism and to some extent the paranormal and not merely the effects of supposedly 'abnormal psychology', which is the reason most often offered by conventional psychiatry to rationalise bizarre occurrences. I do not claim to supply any immediate or profound solutions relating to the causes of these events, because attempts to do so frequently raise more questions than answers, but I can, at least, demonstrate how the subject is regarded in various and, sometimes, quite unexpected quarters.

As we shall see, it is relatively simple and convenient for the scientific establishment to define subjects like mystical and paranormal phenomena using rational explanations then classify them using that definition. Although convenient, this technique does not, and indeed cannot, apply to genuinely anomalous occurrences, because the very definition of the word 'anomalous' means (A) an event occurs for no good or obvious reason in defiance of convention and (B) it cannot be absolutely defined. Religious orthodoxy, however, is faced with something of a dilemma; it is founded on mysticism and is, therefore, obliged to accept the authenticity of 'supernatural' events, which it does, but only on its own tightly defined terms.

I should also emphasise that, when considering the uneasy relationship between religion and the paranormal, I have used the monotheistic faiths rather than pantheistic beliefs to make my case, because the pantheistic faiths are more likely to accept the reality of supernatural events as a natural function of the cosmos. The monotheistic faiths, however, can be extremely selective regarding what they consider as acceptable supernatural and mystical occurrences and tend to allow their own respective dogmas to shape their interpretations. I have chosen to focus on Christianity to illustrate how the fundaments of faith have magickal roots, although this applies equally to Judaism and Islam as well. In fact, it is arguable that Judaism may be even easier to understand in magickal terms, since it long predates Christianity and has an equally mystical system of core values such as the Cabbala etc.

That aside, I made the conscious decision to concentrate on the Roman Catholic version of Christianity in particular, purely on the basis that Roman Catholicism probably has the highest profile within the Christian variations on deism. In addition, the Roman Catholic faith is arguably one of the most mystically inclined in the manner in which it deals with miracles and other related events, although this inclination is clearly shaped by its own dogma. I have, I hasten to add, absolutely no particular quarrel with any religion, providing that it does not attempt to impose its beliefs by diktat and, in the course of what follows, I have used a few extracts from the ancient book, The Holy Bible, although, perhaps, not in the way they were originally intended.

The fact that I have done so may also serve to highlight the commonly-held opinion that the Bible and its many component books can be interpreted in a variety of ways and the same is, of course, true of the Torah and the Qur'an. I had originally intended to write this book with no references to religion whatsoever, but, unfortunately, this proved impossible, because religion and its profoundly mystical/magickal overtones are integral to every culture on the planet in one form or another. It is also at the heart of how they address and reconcile their own religious traditions with the conjoined subjects of supernatural, mystical and magickal phenomena.

Although apparently ambivalent about it, the Roman Catholic Church does accept the reality of its own definition of magick (and always has done, if one considers that it is founded on it) and, in 1489, produced a treatise written by Giovanni Pico della Mirandola setting out its belief that there were two varieties. One was 'Theurgy', or divine magick, and the other, 'Goetia', or demonic magick (one approved and the other condemned and banned). These practices came under what it called 'The Operation of the Stars'. It also recognised the practice of alchemy as 'The Operation of the Sun' and astrology as 'The Operation of the Moon' and both of these disciplines, although viewed with some suspicion, were quite legitimate 'sciences' at that time because they were based on Christian foundations infused with esoteric ideas. Those who chose to follow these routes were accepted as adepts, i.e. alchemists or astrologists who used information gained from secret schools of knowledge and/or 'higher beings' for the glorification of God in particular and the benefit of humanity in general.

It can be difficult to decide whether religion legitimised magick or magick legitimised religion, although logic seems to suggest that it is the second of the two options, because animistic and shamanic traditions long predate any religion and, indeed, were a substitute for it that worked perfectly well. If one casts prejudice aside, it is absolutely obvious that religion and magick are one and the same, because, as they developed and evolved, monotheistic religions did, after all, incorporate many magickal and pagan practices into their respective canons of belief and, through blind dogma, successfully harmonised them using different interpretations. This is particularly true when one considers the ceremonies and rituals used by the Roman Catholic Church as it functions from day to day, rituals that have more than a passing similarity to magickal rites and we will look at some of these in detail later. Where appropriate, I have chosen to use the spelling, 'magick', as opposed to 'magic', the exceptions to this rule are in the word, 'magician', which is spelled in a more conventional manner, because the alternative spelling, 'magickian', seemed awkward. This exception also applies where the source material use the spelling, 'magic'. Why use the variant spelling in the first place? Purely to differentiate between theatrical displays of trickery, conjuring and illusion and genuine instances of deliberately invoked events that defy normal explanations. Of course, this, in turn, begs the question, how does one define magick?

In this case, I decided to define the word by paraphrasing the observation of the magus, Aleister Crowley, who considered magick as the ability to impose one's desires on reality through an act of will alone. This was reflected in his magickal philosophy, which he called 'Thelema', taken from the Greek word for will. There are, of course, alternative ways of looking at this, but this one seems to best encapsulate the concept, since all magickal systems are about causing a change to occur through a variety of deliberate processes and this includes religion. Because of his significance in this matter, the name of Aleister Crowley will appear a number of times in this book. This is also true of important deities such as Jesus Christ.

There is one final point: in the process of writing this book, I frequently had to choose carefully before making decisions and thinking what might be legitimately called 'the unthinkable', because, in the main, tradition, timidity and sheer mental inertia block the pathways to alternative thought. We are brought up in a certain way and our thought processes and values are governed, initially at least, by the influences of parents, school and religion, but, ultimately, by our deep-seated cultural mores and traditions. So effective is this inadvertent brainwashing that taking extremely traditional and conservative values and then standing them on their heads can cause much internal turmoil, but the end result is both rejuvenating and liberating, allowing the individual a much broader perspective, which, in turn, opens many more doors to other possibilities. The more doors one open, the more one finds and the discoveries are fascinating. Hopefully, the contents of this book will cast light in some otherwise dark and noisome places and, by illuminating them, bring freedom.

Chapter 1
Magick and Miracles

In the frequently vexed world of paranormal manifestations, there is one recurring theme and it is this: is there any difference between the magickal displays attributed to saints and other conventionally 'holy people' and those manifested by people such as faith healers, psychics and mediums? Why are the alleged abilities demonstrated by traditional holy men and women adjudged pure and those by the laity the product of 'dark forces', probably demonic in nature? This is a considerably more complex subject than it might, at first, appear, because the talents of those who claim to manifest these talents, especially at will, resonate powerfully with many of the assertions made by organised religions. For reasons best known to the monotheistic faiths in particular, the very mention of paranormal phenomena of any kind, outside their own, narrow definition, is a complete anathema and the very existence of such non-approved events is denied and rejected.

It is likely that the rejection stems from two factors: (1) the events outside the direct control of officially-sanctioned religious bodies are effectively 'extracurricular' and cannot be regulated according to their wishes; (2) they guard their own manifestations of magick and mysticism very jealously indeed and this includes miraculous or 'spirit' healing; (3) it might allow their flock to actually think for themselves. The second factor applies especially to the rituals, rites and ceremonies of the Roman Catholic faith and its unswerving acceptance of, for example, transubstantiation, where the bread and wine consecrated during the Eucharist of Holy Mass transforms into the body and blood of Christ in the solemn ritual that ends in Holy Communion. This practice clearly infers that Christ is physically present on the altar for a period of time. A close variant of this belief is also found in the Anglican faith, but, in this case, it is called 'consubstantiation'. The same concept recurs in a later chapter, but this time associated with a much, much darker context.

This interpretation sounds rather like the very similar assertion that we, the human race, are made in God's image and likeness. When this statement is challenged, the usual response is that we should not interpret it literally, i.e. in any physical sense, although some do, but that the likeness is entirely spiritual. This, of course, removes a heavy burden of proof from those who hold this view, but it is one of the most accessible examples concerning scripture and how to interpret it. In terms of religious iconography, depictions of the Christian God are almost always of some Zeus-like figure sitting in splendour among the clouds, observing and judging what occurs in the Earth beneath. It is graphic, simple, easily-accessible and creates an immediate bond between the faithful and the object of that faith. It is the same rationalisation that allowed great artists and sculptors to anthropomorphise the concept of magickal creatures like angels. This was a situation that suited the Church well, because it allowed the faithful to identify more intimately with these supernatural entities as something tangible, rather than a hypothetical intermediary between them and God that existed purely on someone's say so. It should be added that, in Islam, images of God/Allah are explicitly forbidden and regarded as blasphemy, because Muslims consider Allah to be perfect and, since humans are manifestly not, any attempt to portray him are bound to be imperfect.

These are not, by any means, the only examples of anomalous phenomena to populate the canon of Church dogma. The other obvious examples of mystical and magickal occurrences within, once again, the Catholic Church, include visions of the Blessed Virgin Mary (BVM), miraculous healing, levitation, weeping statues, prophesy, bilocation and, of course, the rather disquieting phenomenon of stigmata. None of these manifestations are, by any definition, normal or conventional and must, therefore, be regarded as 'paranormal' or something that exists in parallel with what is considered normal. However, in this case, the Church teaches that if the examples quoted above stem from the Holy Spirit, they are, therefore, acceptable. These events do still occur from time to time, especially examples of healing, weeping statues and, much more rarely, stigmata, i.e. the spontaneous appearance of the wounds inflicted on Christ during His death by crucifixion.

In the main, these marks appear spontaneously on particularly pious individuals, although this has not always been the case. While willing to accept that events like these sometimes occur, in fairness to the Church, it does demand stringent measures of proof, drawn from various sources, before it will even consider their validity. This is especially true when they are claimed to have happened due to the invocation of, or intercession by, a particularly pious and devout member of its flock. An excellent example of this is demonstrated on a daily basis at Lourdes, when the ailing faithful (and not always Roman Catholic, either) arrive in the hope of obtaining a miraculous cure from whatever ailment afflicts them.

In term of numbers, recent estimates put the numbers of sick who go on a pilgrimage to Lourdes seeking a cure at approximately 80,000 people per annum (excluding helpers). This pilgrimage has been occurring for almost one hundred years now and, when the maths are done, this makes for almost eight million seriously-ill people who have taken part and of that eight million faithful, there have been fewer that seventy attested 'miracles'. None of these miracles have, for example, involved the re-growth of a limb or any missing or severely-damaged organ and have been confined solely to medical conditions. Apart from Lourdes, these events occur elsewhere and when attributed to an individual, normally deceased, if they occur in sufficient numbers, they frequently contribute to the process leading to the eventual canonisation of that person prior to their elevation to sainthood.

One of the more recent examples of this has already begun, following the beatification of the late Pope John Paul II (the first step in the procedure). Another person in the final stages of canonisation is Padre Pio, a noted Italian Capuchin monk, who was also a mystic and stigmatic. Perhaps it might be unfair to make the observation that people who actually do pray for relief or, better still, a cure from some medical condition and find that it occurs, might be receiving this from an as yet unknown function within the human body itself. Bear in mind that the normally sceptical medical profession does recognise that 'spontaneous remission' occurs when people displaying symptoms of a variety of conditions are suddenly 'cured', sometimes literally overnight and for no good or obvious reason. Let us be clear about instances of healing approved by the Church. Although it does accept, welcome and condone proven instances of healing as a sign of God's grace, it does so with less complacency than in earlier times. This came about in the Middle Ages, during the plagues that ravaged much of Europe, when it became obvious that the plague was no respecter of the faithful and infected them as readily as it did the irreligious. Prayer, it seemed, was no defence against disease.

Does a spontaneous remission qualify as a miracle? The only difference here is that no invocation is made to a higher power and if the cure is medically verifiable then what mechanism brought it about? Might this also mean that those claiming a cure from illness brought about by prayers to a saint, whether verified or not, may also have inadvertently triggered this self-healing function? Could this legitimately be described as magickal? Another possibility might be that, since we are surrounded by invisible and normally inaccessible energy fields, those who have experienced inexplicable cures from whatever source might even have unwittingly utilised these to effect a physical cure at the atomic level. This may even have some scientific basis, because researchers have now isolated a human gene, defined as 'p21', which appears to inhibit the ability to rebuild tissue. Deliberately deactivating this gene may eventually lead to astonishing medical breakthroughs in the natural and spontaneous replacement of human organs in the same way that newts can re-grow tails etc.

Might this mean that, in some cases, the information encoded into the human DNA molecule can, somehow, temporarily override or rewrite its programme to effect these apparently miraculous cures, but only in a limited fashion? This, of course, brings us right back to the question of why and how? More questions with more (albeit speculative) answers, but it might mean that the human brain is able to react to specific situations in ways that have not yet even been considered and exert influences over the very atomic structure of the human body and the elements that form it. If this can be effectively and positively demonstrated at some time in the future, would it mean that yet another brick in the edifice of religious belief has been removed? Finally, if the welcome possibility of gene-related cures at some time in the future can be ignored, could it mean that the 'spiritual power' to which the faithful attribute these miracles also hands out 'freebies' to those it considers deserving? There are no hard and fast rules here, because these cures can and do occur and the rush to ascribe them to saints etc. may be an oversimplification of what has actually happened.

Evidence of spontaneous remission aside, while belief in miracles is prevalent in all religions, it appears to have greater support within the Catholic Church, which is, of course, an extremely influential and powerful organisation with global reach. It is also an organisation that sees absolutely no dichotomy between accepting one instance of the supernatural, which it displays on a daily basis during the ritual of The Mass and other more credible (in terms of documented evidence) examples of mystical phenomena. As if that were not enough, in keeping with the thoughts of the aforementioned Giovanni Pico della Mirandola, the difference is justified by adding the provision that anything that does not appear to originate from God (by definition, good) must, therefore, stem from Satanic or demonic sources (by definition, evil). This vital difference, therefore, automatically proscribes any form of unofficial communication with the 'other side'.

Although obviously not nearly as oppressive as in the Dark and Middle Ages, when heresy was defined as anything that the Church did not sanction or approve of, at present, science, particularly in the field of DNA research, and the possibilities it holds, is still viewed with particular suspicion. This is because of the way in which the Church defines the reproductive process, especially the point at which life begins, and was founded centuries before the sciences of genetics, DNA stem cell research and embryology were even thought of. While on the subject of miracles, I fully accept that these fortuitous events can and do occur, it is the reasons why, however, that are open to question. It is an old cliché to attribute what occurs to some hitherto unsuspected function of the mind, but as our understanding of what the human brain is capable steadily increases and we continue to unlock the secrets of human DNA and the interaction between the two, perhaps this, too, will eventually be revealed. It may also reveal much about how magick functions.

There is one more factor to consider here and it is purely pragmatic: spontaneous remission or a poorly understood function inherent in the human condition. Both are possible means by which healing might occur, but there is, of course, another. If someone who is ill does respond positively to the effects generated by a prayer (or a spell, which is arguably the same thing) offered by someone they have approached for help, can they, or anyone else, be sure that this is what actually cured them? If it was only a sheer coincidence, but these coincidences became increasingly focused around what one individual was doing, then it does tend to point to something very odd taking place, but even that does not really matter, as long as this person continues to make these events happen.

The interest then automatically turns not just to the cure, but to its source. What about the person who regularly made these cures happen? If this did not involve giving any potions or pills, but seemed to occur through an act of will, then what are they doing? On one level, this is a legitimate and, indeed, vital area for research and a possible goldmine of useful information, although, as with any cure, no doubt those in receipt of the benefits would not really care how it happened, but it does not answer the underlying question, why? Unfortunately, this is a circular argument that always returns to the basic premise: if it is not pills and potions and it is not prayer that causes these events to occur, then what unknown mechanism brings them about? Perhaps, as we venture further along this path, some answers may emerge.

One thing that should be made clear from the outset is the difference between approved 'spirit healing' and non-approved 'spiritualist healing', because the two, although they might achieve identical results, are not the same. The latter implies a link with the dead and faith is secondary and, as such, merges with the occult and, not surprisingly, it is specifically forbidden by the Church in Deuteronomy 18:9-18. On the other hand, it could also be argued that 'spirit healing' has nothing to do with religious belief and more about interacting with and harmonising the 'life essence' of the patient. This is sometimes expressed as 'soul' or 'spirit', yet neither description fully covers what is occurring nor describes the nature of the energy involved. As we shall see, the attitude of the Church to healing, irrespective of how it is achieved, is both inconsistent and hypocritical. Hopefully, what is contained in these pages may help demystify this, along with the other points raised, and demonstrate that the ability to alter reality, whether in relation to healing or any other manifestation of magick, on some level, at least, is innate in all of humanity, providing the will is present.

Before leaving this chapter, we should consider an anomaly, i.e. the reasons why paintings and other examples of artworks depicting Christ, his family and all those associated with Him never show them as other than western and European in appearance. Depictions of Christ, especially in the cinema, have shown him with blond hair and blue eyes or dark-haired with blue eyes, in fact, anything other than what he would have looked like. There are few, if any, actual descriptions of Christ in scripture and those that are there are sketchy, to say the least. He has been variously described as small with a hunched back and also as a cripple, certainly not as a tall, handsome, light-skinned Caucasian male.

The same is true of his mother, the Blessed Virgin Mary, who is always shown as fair-skinned woman. In fact, it could even be said that the various visions of the BVM reported at Fatima, Lourdes, Medjugorje and the other sites where she has, supposedly, manifested are invariably of a beautiful, radiant, fair-skinned woman. Does this mean that the Holy Family can appear in whatever form or colour they wish, so as to more closely identify with the country in which they manifest? Or, as is more likely, is this a product of the Westernised faith that Christianity has become? It is strange that these whole body materialisations have yet to occur in Africa or China or, indeed, America, but if they did, it is a safe bet that they would conform to the accepted image. The fact is that the Holy Family were Semitic and lived in a Semitic country, therefore they would have been dark or swarthy in colour and to present them in any other way is patently false. This would, however, not suit the Western faithful, who have grown up with the Western version of Jesus and it would be educational to see the reaction to such an occurrence.

Chapter 2
Magick Within the Bible

If we can accept the notion that supernatural events are examples of magick, whether they are approved by the Church or otherwise, then we can look at some occurrences that are described in both testaments of the Bible. One of the most dramatic is the opening of the Red Sea, as Moses led his people to safety from the predations of Pharaoh's army. Scripture says that Moses stood and commanded the waters to open to allow his flock safe passage to the other side and the waters were, indeed, opened and his people did arrive safely on the other shore. However, when the Egyptian army followed in hot pursuit, the waters crashed around their ears and drowned them: the power of God or something else? It also gives good cause to ask if Moses was a shaman or a magician, which leads us into the slightly uneasy arena of so-called 'words of power'.

The word of power supposedly used by Moses to cause the waters of the Red Sea to recede and part was the Shemhamforash or 'pre-eminent name of God', consisting of 72 syllables. The word itself derives from the Book of Exodus by taking three of its verses, each containing 72 letters to create a further 72 three-letter names of God. The use of the word was also used in the manufacture of a golem, the terrifying artificial being of legend in the Jewish faith. The tale of the golem might also be seen as an analogy based on the creation of the first man, Adam, because, according to scriptural tradition, Adam was created from dust into which God breathed life and the golem is also created, in the main, from earth and then activated by a rabbi using the real name of God.

Traditional magickal belief holds that once you posses the true or secret name of a person or thing, then you possess power over it and, if you were to obtain the secret (or ineffable) name of God, then you could use it to wield unimaginable power, simply because anything done using His secret name would leave Him, like it or not, with no option other than to obey you. This is where religion and one of the 'old religions', in this case nature worship/Wicca, agree. The secret name of God is usually expressed as the Tetragrammaton, YHVH (YOD, HEY, VAU, HEY) and considered a 'safe' manner in which to use this name, due to possible dire repercussions visited on the user should something go even slightly wrong. Some of the more fundamentalist opinions considered it unwise to even think the name.

Another example of biblical magick is, of course, the Ark of the Covenant, used by the Hebrews to talk to God. The Ark is credited with a unique power and place in biblical history, based upon various scriptural quotations that God Himself actually spoke from a cloud above the mercy seat atop the Ark, as revealed in Leviticus 16:2, Numbers 7:89 and Exodus 25:22. Therefore, in addition to its purpose as a repository for the Ten Commandments, it also apparently served as a spiritual communications device, similar to that which Noah used on his Ark. According to the Bible, in Exodus 25: 17-22 and 37: 1-9, the Ark itself was made on the specific instructions of God to the following measurements: 2½ cubits long, 1½ cubits wide and 1½ cubits high and fashioned of wood and metal, in this case, durable shittim (acacia) wood and gold. The removable lid of the Ark (called the mercy seat) was surmounted by two kneeling angels (cherubim) with wings outstretched towards one another, all made of solid gold and the box section was constructed of acacia, covered with gold sheets. The box section was also fitted with a ring at each corner so that poles could be inserted to carry it. Along with the construction details came a stern warning that, upon pain of death, the Ark should not be touched nor even looked into by anyone not ordained to do so. Is this an example of biblical magick or is it something else entirely?

Wicca and The Christian Church

The secret words of Wicca, a magickal system of nature worship conceived by the late Gerald Gardener, involve the hidden names of the Horned God and Goddess, which are regarded as a secret only imparted to initiates. One of the really bizarre coincidences that indicate similarities between the beliefs of Wicca with those of Christianity is the origin and nature of the Horned God. It is a comparison that will never be openly acknowledged by the Christian faith, but may well be acceptable in Wicca. Wicca is a duotheistic religion that, although nature-based and sharing some gnostic concepts, does require a godhead to worship, although it opts for the much more sensible approach of having a female counterpart as well. The Horned God of nature has been variously interpreted as Herne the Hunter, Robin Goodfellow, Janus, Tammuz and Damuzi, Cernunos, Pan, Pashupati, Dionysus, Green Jack, The Green Man and all the way back to Osiris. He has even been considered as a forerunner of the semi-mythical hero figure of Robin Hood.

From this selection of names, we find a range of traditions encompassing those of Celtic, Greek, Roman, Indian and Egyptian origin, so it is a concept deeply embedded in the human psyche, almost hard-wired, in fact, and has been for millennia. The nature of the Horned God also appears to have an element of 'shape shifting' about it, because there are cave paintings and other very early depictions of this entity showing him as half-man and half-stag or, in the case of Pan, as half-man, half-goat, all designed to emphasise libido and fertility. It is these early cave paintings of therianthropic (i.e. half-man, half-animal and, sometimes, half-man, half-insect) beings that give hints that these beliefs were around anywhere between thirty to forty thousand years ago, the images in the caves at Lascaux in France being a case in point. It is also possible that the tales of centaurs came about through crossovers from similar ancient sources. The Herne the Hunter variant casts him as giant with his head adorned with massive antlers, an interpretation that is uniquely British and, in this tradition, he is regarded as the leader of the 'wild hunt'.

Occasional reports of sightings of Herne still emerge from Windsor Great Park in England, where legend has it that he still exists to this day. This has curious resonances with the very occasional present-day tales concerning sightings of Bigfoot, the Sasquatch and other man/beast halflings from remote forests around the world. It is thought that the longevity of this particular character stems from the already mentioned worship of Cernunos (or Cernuous, the spellings vary) and still finds an outlet in Robin Hood, who's father, according to some traditions, was Herne. In fact, the cult of Herne the Hunter was so powerful and far-reaching that the fledgling Christian Church did everything it could to discourage the belief and eventually adopted the image of Herne into their own canon of belief as the deo falsus or false God, i.e. the Devil. It is an interpretation that squares well with the ancient legends that Herne was also the Lord of the Underworld, something that he shared with the Egyptian traditions of Osiris. The creation of the Devil was a logical development, designed to emphasise the sanctity, purity and basic goodness of the Christian God; where there is good, there must also be evil, otherwise the idea of goodness has nothing with which to compare it.

The Goddess figure and the partner of the Horned God, is often portrayed in three and, sometimes, four phases. She is the Moon to Herne's Sun; she is the Maiden, the Mother, the Crone and, rather disconcertingly, sometimes 'The Dark'. These coincide with the four seasons of spring, summer, autumn and winter and can also be aligned with phases of the Moon. None of these definitions is intended to be an insult, but are instead designed to show the vibrancy, compassion and wisdom of the female principal. It is the female principal that governs many Wiccan circles and although men do participate, there are other Wiccan groups dedicated to Diana that are the sole preserve of females. The origins of Christ also draw on such ancient God figures as Tammuz, Horus, Krishna, Mithras and on to, once again, Osiris. One was concerned with fertility and the other was a sun god, one depends on the other to thrive and both are vital to the human race and, consequently, there is frequently some overlap. Strictly speaking, we should be cautious about including Osiris in this panoply of deities, because as well as being associated with the Sun, he was also a traditional corn god, but, either way, he was associated with growth and renewal.

As regards the use of the names of individual deities, on one hand there is a clear proscription on using the name of the God of monotheism as a magickal word of power, irrespective of which version is used, which, according to ancient Hebrew texts, is a crime punishable by stoning. The same warning, minus the threat of stoning, is also given in one of the Ten Commandments where, 'Thou shalt not take the name of the Lord thy God in vain', and it is categorical with no ifs or buts. Yet, in Hindu traditions (which admittedly is not monotheist), it is positively encouraged as an act of veneration, resulting in the rhythmic chants of 'Hare Krishna'. A much less spectacular, but just as effective, example of biblical magick was seen during the wedding feast at Canaan, when Jesus, at the request of His mother, is supposed to have changed water into wine when supplies started to run low.

There are, of course, many other examples of biblical magick, e.g. the feeding of the five thousand, the burning bush, walking on water and calming the storm in the Sea of Galilee. All magickal events and all designed to demonstrate how Jesus was drawing His power from God - either that or He was a truly mighty magician, more of which later. In fact, as we have seen, the subjects of magick or magickal occurrences are common throughout both testaments of the Bible. Two further examples are Moses and Aaron who had staffs that could be turned into snakes [Exodus 7:8-13] as did the staff used by the sorcerer of the Pharaoh, all clear signs of God's dominance over the serpent/Satan and basic demonstrations of good always besting evil. This produces yet another resonance with ancient legends concerning the magickal staffs allegedly employed in building the pyramids.

This is an area of study dotted with pitfalls, but these legends describe a remarkable device called the 'Staff of Ra', which was allegedly used by the Egyptian priests, who presumably were permanently on site at the time, to allow the huge blocks of stone to be manoeuvred into place. The legends say that, prior to the heavy blocks being moved, the priest struck the stone block a sharp blow with the staff, causing it to vibrate at a very high frequency. This, apparently, rendered it virtually weightless and allowed it to be moved with relative ease. This story, although unprovable, is typical of the legends that grew up around this enormous, ancient civil engineering project and whether it is true or not comes second to the fact that the project was ever completed at all. As regards the staff, assuming that it existed at all, it seems reasonable to suppose that, given the sheer scale of the undertaking, there would need to be more than one of them and more than one person with the knowledge to use them. Might this be described as magick or a type of lost technology?

One theory championed by an American engineer, Tom Danley, also postulates that the stones were 'floated' into place using a technique he calls 'sonic levitation'. Danley has studied this technology, which is based on earlier pioneering work with infrasound, carried out over a period of years during the 1950s by French researcher, Vladimir Gavreau. In the case of Gavreau, the use of infrasound was developed with military applications in mind. Various governments still conduct covert infrasound projects as part of so-called 'non-lethal' weapons programs and there is every reason to believe that they are routinely used as part of crowd control measures. Danley believes that a much earlier version of this technology was employed by the ancient Egyptians to vibrate the stone blocks at a high frequency, thereby rendering them effectively weightless.

According to Danley's painstaking research, there are even hieroglyphic carvings that corroborate the existence of the mysterious 'Staff of Ra' and indicate that this device was, indeed, used to make the blocks of stone weightless. Remarkable as this suggestion might be, there is an even more bizarre (and magickal) function attributed to the pyramids. Danley took sound measurements within the Great Pyramid, also known as the Cheops Pyramid or the Pyramid of Khufu, using amplifiers and speakers located in the series of so-called 'relieving chambers' above the King's Chamber. After measuring the resultant standing frequency, 16Hz, which is below the range of human hearing, he found that it corresponded to the F# chord. Based on this discovery, the purpose of the cavities above the King's Chamber, originally assumed to have been constructed to alleviate the structural stresses within the pyramid, may have had an entirely different function. Their purpose may have been to deliberately 'tune' the structure to a specific frequency. Like other ancient civilisations, the Egyptians instinctively recognised this frequency as a harmonic of the planet, although they may not have fully appreciated that the entire cosmos exists in a range of frequencies.

Danley also speculates that when the original limestone cladding was in place and the sides of the pyramid were smooth, the wind blowing over the entrances to the small, so-called 'aligning shafts' that penetrate into the pyramid would create a musical note, similar to that produced by blowing over the neck of a bottle (a phenomenon called Helmholtz resonance). Yet another magickal connection is evident with the witch-doctors and shamans of indigenous North American tribes who tuned their ceremonial flutes to... yes, F#. How did another race, separated by thousands of miles in distance and centuries in time, come to the same conclusion? In fact, this frequency is entrained in the very fabric of the Earth, so what fundamental truth is demonstrated here? There is every possibility that this essential commonality stretches back for millions of years and, while this surely cannot have been the only reason for constructing the pyramids, it does appear to be a factor encapsulated within them.

All of this long predates any kind of modern monotheistic religion and, indeed, any concept of a Creator God, but it does demonstrate a remarkable degree of affinity with the planet and an understanding of how things worked. Once again, is this magick or very early and also instinctive examples of technology that we cannot fully replicate? Whether or not the priests of ancient Egypt were able to produce the results claimed using a 'staff' is a moot point, but if they had, then it is almost certain that the name of one of their pantheon of gods would have been invoked in the process as a word of power, whether it was needed or not. This, of course, once again goes straight to the question of whether this was an early example of a highly-complex technology or a startling example of magick and also serves to demonstrate the axiom of the late visionary author, Arthur C Clarke, that any sufficiently advanced (or, indeed, in this case, sufficiently ancient) technology is indistinguishable from magick.

This brings us back to the staffs used by Aaron and Moses and the Staff of Ra. The same principle lies behind the magick wands used by various types of wizard, sorcerer and shaman, where it acts as a focus or channel for the forces they summon, while also serving the purpose of singling them out as in some way special; perhaps a badge indicating their status. Although many examples of this type of magick are cited, it is possible that these are not actually magick, but incorrect interpretations of heretical practices. In addition, magickal rites were often associated with the worship of Baal, which could be one of many Semitic deities or even the mythical sun god of the Phoenicians. At a later date, this changed slightly and it became the standard belief that all magick was demonic in nature and, therefore, even more undesirable and so it remained and, for the most part, still does to this present day.

Islam and Judaism also mention magickal practices and entities. One example of this occurs when King Solomon (Sulayman), who was also a demonologist of some note, built his temple and used a number of demons, supposedly forty, to assist in the project. As far as their use by Solomon goes, one of the early works describing how to summon and control them is the legendary 'grimoire' (book of spells) entitled, The Testament of Solomon the King and there is another related volume called the Lemegeton. According to the Talmud, there are a total of 7,405,962 demons, all with different names and functions. It is curious to note that the origins of the word 'demon' rather than describing a symbol of everything evil, can also be translated from the Greek to mean 'genius' or 'teacher' and this has immense implications regarding their purpose in the order of things. There is more information of grimoires and their contents at the end of this book. Incidentally, Islam also recognises the reality of demons, but calls then jinn, jinni or, sometimes, djinn.

Other examples of religious magick can be found in the still common belief that holy artefacts and trinkets associated with saints etc. are assumed to have the transferred ability to effect cures. Sometimes these objects are fragments of clothing or small items once worn by the person whose magickal/divine aid is requested. On other occasions, these items consist of actual body parts from various sacred cadavers. It was a cynical practice that proved an excellent source of income for some of the less scrupulous Crusaders who brought back bales of supposed relics from the Holy Lands.

These took the form of everything from parts of the 'true cross' to dubious fragments of bone and scraps of desiccated flesh, allegedly from long-dead saints.

Transferred or Sympathetic Magick

The largely uneducated, gullible and superstitious laity eagerly bought the looted items for their supposedly curative and protective abilities and the practice even went so far as to touch other items with these supposedly 'holy relics' in the assumption that the powers inherent in the original relic would somehow transfer to the other item. Nails from the 'true cross' (and there were a surprisingly large number of them) were reduced to iron filings to be later incorporated into other metallic items, each thought to possess some of the powers of the original. Modern versions of these customs can still be found at the launch of ships, where the invocation that God should bless the vessel and all who sail in it is made. It is also regularly seen when someone is 'touched for luck' should they win a raffle, lottery or other competition.

A rather more worrying example of this type of 'transferred magick' occurred during the rallies held in support of the Nazi Party in Germany prior to the start of the Second World War, where Adolph Hitler 'christened' the banners of various Nazi groups by touching then with the so-called 'Blood Banner'. This banner was a flag used at one of the early rabble rousing meetings that ended up with the then fledgling Nazi Party being routed by the German authorities. The banner became an important symbol of the enduring qualities of Nazi doctrine and may even hint at the occult leanings that are regularly associated with Hitler and his philosophy. Again, it would be simple to ascribe any cures or other effects apparently caused by these objects to simple luck or coincidence, but here, once again, we find this strange 'coincidence factor' occurring. As before, if 'coincidences' start grouping around one particular artefact then it becomes increasingly difficult to rationalise them as pure chance. If the item is also considered as 'holy' then, according to the faithful, this is obviously the work of the all-seeing, all-beneficent God being channelled through the artefact via the intercession of a saint and, in the absence of any other obvious factor, this is understandable.

On the other hand, if the artefact was dedicated to some other deity, one of the Old Gods or perhaps even Satan and it still produced remarkable coincidences, then there has to be another unknown factor involved. It is here that we start to confront the possibilities opened up by the power inherent in the human mind. If cures and healing can be occasioned by the invocation of a range of deities, be they 'holy' or 'unholy', then this must indicate some other factor that has no relationship to the object or deity of veneration involved and this possibility will be explored in the following chapters.

Chapter 3
Magick, Levitation and The Rapture

There is, however, an example of spiritual magick mentioned above which is virtually unheard of now and that is spontaneous levitation, where the body of the entranced person rises from wherever they are and floats, unsupported, in mid-air. Occasionally, this used to involve someone, normally a particularly pious saint, actually travelling for a short distance through air and returning to their point of origin. For some reason, this no longer happens or, at least, instances of it are no longer reported, although apparent displays of levitation were regularly demonstrated by such psychic mediums as Daniel Dunglas Home during the heyday of the Spiritualist movement. The more one examines this particular manifestation of the paranormal (or perhaps it might better be described as magick), it actually matters less that the individuals involved were able to manifest the feat, but more about the mechanism behind it.

That said, the idea of being lifted bodily into the air, whether by one's own efforts or those of some outside source, is accepted as a matter of faith by certain fundamentalist Evangelical and Pentecostal Christian believers. It is these groups who accept the Bible as the literal, revealed word of God, rather than the mixture of history, allegory, metaphor, magick and fable that it actually is. Unlikely as it might seem, these believers are absolutely convinced that the idea of physical levitation is a given, only they call it 'The Rapture', and when the End Times come and the Antichrist emerges, they, and they alone, will be raised up into the air to remain in safety while the rest of humanity suffers in what they call 'The Tribulation'. The number designated for salvation is, for reasons best known to the believers, remarkably specific at 144,000.

They base their beliefs on the following biblical prophesy: Thessalonians 4:16-17 says, "And the dead in Christ will rise first: then we who are alive, who are left, shall be caught up together with them in the clouds to meet the Lord in the air, and so we shall always be with the Lord." They see nothing odd or unusual about this and actively embrace it as a received truth. In fact, it draws a parallel with the Islamic belief that the faithful who die in the service of Allah will live forever more in Allah's garden and every whim will be attended to by seventy beautiful virgins. Although one fate is rather more pragmatic and earthy than the other, they do both allude to war and strife as the backdrop of their salvation. Despite the fact that the ethos for both belief systems is one of humility and peace, they do, in fact, feature war and combat in their structure, i.e. "Onward Christian soldiers marching off to war" and, of course, the bloodthirsty religious battles of the Crusades.

Continuing on the perverse themes of war and eventual salvation, shortly after The Tribulation comes Armageddon, when the armies of Heaven battle the forces of Satan and the Antichrist on the plains of Megiddo in Israel. Once the forces of light win (and, evidently, this is another given that has abundantly clear, supernatural and magickal overtones) and Satan is safely locked away, those who had been Raptured will return to live in a 'heaven on Earth'. However, there is still more to come and one thousand years after Armageddon, Satan escapes from capture and, once again, challenges the forces of light. This time, the Earth itself is destroyed, but a new one descends from the heavens and, at long last, there is everlasting and eternal peace. After this mayhem, with its precursor of mass levitations, what was the mechanism that brought it all about? Unfortunately, as with the levitating saints, the answer is 'the power of God', which needs no explanation whatsoever. All of this seems to indicate that the Bible, instead of the revealed word of Almighty God, might equally be a treatise on magick, which is another idea that occurs again later.

The same is also true when one encounters the claims of levitation exhibited by those who are in the thrall of Satanic and/or demonic forces. It is a fairly standard ploy used in cinematic representations of demonic possession where the individual who is possessed is levitated into the air and then set back down again. Logic suggests that the mechanism must be the same, but one is approved (the power of God) and the other is not (the power of Satan). In both cases, what is demonstrated is clearly an example of magick, but, for some reason, this is the word that dare not speak its name, although, to mark the difference between the two powers, anything purporting to come from God might be referred to as 'white magick' and from Satan as 'black magick'.

The same is true in such influential fictional literary works as the Lord of The Rings trilogy, where there is a 'white wizard', Gandalf, and his evil (ergo 'black wizard') counterpart, Sauron. The similarities between the Gandalf/Christ-Sauron/Satan imagery are also striking in that, in his efforts to protect his flock, he is initially killed by the forces of Sauron, but later returns in all his glory to vanquish the might of the dark empire. It is also notable that the forces of evil are portrayed as uniformly hideous and unspeakably brutal. On the other hand, those under the protection of Gandalf are seen as naïve, loyal, kindly and well-meaning and backed up by elemental forces that, for the most part, are either semi- or wholly-magickal. Neither is it an accident that the name, Sauron, is chosen because of its obvious connection to the world of reptiles (saurians) and Satan is often referred to as 'that old dragon'. In spite of these semantic considerations, the only place that hard parallels like this can be made is in the world of allegory and fiction, because representatives of all the mainstream religions balk at the very thought that miracles, because of negative associations, could possibly be defined as magick.

There is a third order of phenomena which is rarely mentioned in this context and that is what supposedly happens during alien abduction scenarios when the abductee is 'levitated' into, presumably, non-terrestrial spacecraft. Does this count as magick or is this an example of the kind of 'spiritual technology' that might have been used by the Egyptians we encountered earlier? It does, however, give rise to serious consideration of alleged levitations attributed to saints and other assorted holy people and the claims made about the Rapture. This particular area tends to blur the boundaries between religion, magick and some of the more left-field versions of ufology, where the believers are sure that levitation and the Rapture are a misinterpretation of their own technology-based paradigm. These particular believers are sure that, prior to 'the end', the human race will, indeed, be lifted up in its entirety (and not just a chosen few) from the face of the Earth, but in a fleet of giant spacecraft.

These spacecraft are, evidently, already here on permanent standby and are currently parked in orbit around the Moon, but they are 'cloaked' and, therefore, invisible. In this version of the myth, rather than the forces of darkness, viz. Satan and the Antichrist, ranged against those of light, viz. Christ, there are two races of extraterrestrials fighting over the Earth and its population. This is a hypothesis that, when one looks at it, runs accepted wisdom a pretty close parallel. The only differences are in the context and the end results are, of course, rather different. This version of events has the friendly ETs (blond, tall, blue-eyed 'Nordics', a clear parallel with angels) in combat with the non-friendly ETs (nasty, reptilian beings, the comparison with demons is not difficult to make) over the fate of humanity. However, humanity is conveniently well out of the way aboard these truly gigantic spacecraft and the outcome is a forgone conclusion. The 'good' ETs defeat the 'bad' ETs and humanity either returns to the Earth or travels with the 'good' ETs to their idyllic home worlds (Heaven).

It is clear that nothing changes and it is a paradigm that is hard-wired into the human psyche, for there is only so much that the downtrodden and oppressed can take until a hero figure emerges to lead them to safety and security. Once again, this 'hero figure' can take many forms, mostly male, but, in a few instances, female. The hero/heroine normally undertakes some onerous task that risks life and limb, sometimes gets killed, but, frequently, is reborn unscathed and always with the purpose of their mission achieved. It does not matter whether this mission is the salvation of humanity or the rescue of a single person, neither does it matter how long the odds are, good invariably prevails over evil and usually with some degree of supernatural assistance. In fact, it can be no other way, good must always triumph over evil, just as a light must always overcome the dark. It does not matter that, for a brief time at least, the forces of evil seem invincible and all-powerful and millions suffer as a consequence, because, somewhere in the chaos and mayhem, the seeds of hope are sown and from these few seeds grows the source of 'pure spirit' that will one day restore the balance.

Chapter 4
The Scientific Paradigm

Here we come to the first of many glaring inconsistencies. Religious beliefs of one kind or another are held by much of the world's population, to a point where the morality and ethos in individual cultures, societies and, indeed, that of entire countries is based on religious and, therefore, unprovable tenets and beliefs. Unfortunately, some of these countries are theocracies where divine rule is absolute and unforgiving. Enforcement criteria aside, this presents another interesting contradiction. On one hand, there are supposedly logical and objective scientists who reject the existence of anything remotely connected with psi or, indeed, paranormal phenomena in general, yet, at the same time, many of these self-same scientists espouse belief in a Creator God and see nothing amiss in this.

Another factor in this as far, as science is concerned, is that magick is grievously flawed because it does not obey or run to a given set of laws. Science expects and demands rationality and, unfortunately, magick is not rational. Therefore, in spite of the fact that it seems to work, as Sir James Frazer says in his seminal masterwork, The Golden Bough, "Magic is the bastard sister of science, it is therefore a truism, almost a tautology, to say that magic is necessarily false and barren, for were it ever to become true and fruitful, it would no longer be magic but science." This statement is vindicated by Arthur C Clarke's previously mentioned (and paraphrased) observation, made many decades later, that one man's technology is another man's magick. Even this insightful definition might be slightly wide of the mark as far as the truth is concerned. Perhaps it is better to keep the three subjects in discrete and parallel paths with magick settling into its natural location separating the two polar opposites, but still accessible to both and, more importantly, to those who choose to practice it.

This is what the Church was (and still is) terrified of and why it remains deeply suspicious of anything that threatens its grip on power. As we will see a little later, it is why it launched its lengthy, brutal and ruthless attack on anything it perceived as heresy and a deviation from its brittle dogma. One thing that neither side seems able or willing to admit is that while religion has had little or no effect at all on science, science has had a major effect on religion and this is something we will find repeatedly as our journey continues. One especially telling example of this was when Galileo was hounded for daring to suggest that the Earth went around the Sun, rather than the other way round. This persecution came directly from the Church's view that since God had put the human race at the centre of the universe, then it was obvious that the Sun had to revolve around the Earth. This was called a 'heliocentric' doctrine.

This interpretation came about because of the artificial boundaries based upon ignorance and superstition that had been placed on scientific research. From our present day perspective, the reason for this is quite obvious: when science establishes, beyond any doubt, that some item of scripture is demonstrably wrong, e.g. the heliocentric nature of the universe or the entire Creation myth, then it would be foolish to defend the situation. Sadly, in some areas, especially in the Bible Belt of the USA, there are the deluded few who insist that The Creation is a literal truth simply because it says so in the Bible and they have gone to remarkable and, ultimately, flawed lengths attempting to prove their hypothesis. Fortunately, this is still a free world, so despite the abundant evidence to the contrary, they are allowed to continue with their beliefs, but this could have potentially dangerous outcomes and, at worst, could see us thrust back into a latter day Dark Age of fear and superstition. Hopefully that day will never come.

As with those whose sole function is to promote religion, how can someone with a supposedly rational background accept one variety of the supernatural as valid yet reject another? Might this be attributable to expediency or sheer pragmatism and nothing else? Examined from another perspective, all monotheistic belief is promoted and directed by a hierarchy of representatives who, presumably, accept their own philosophy unquestioningly, although there are almost certainly at least a few who continually wrestle with self-doubt. Be that as it may, while proclaiming their belief in a Creator God in one form or another, as we have seen, these ecclesiastics also ostensibly reject the existence of 'non-standard' paranormal phenomena. It is also curious how some adherents of individual faiths absolutely reject the validity of others. Since ecumenism is still strongly resisted within certain schisms (normally Protestant fundamentalist) in the Christian congregation, how can any meaningful degree of understanding ever be achieved between different religions?

Although this attitude is less than helpful, nevertheless there are preachers from all religious persuasions who will freely, albeit off the record, admit such as the truth that we do make contact with those who have gone before, but admonish that this is not something that should be done lightly and preferably not at all. This bizarre, but unofficial, melding of beliefs seems to indicate that science and religion have formed an unholy alliance to maintain their own version of the status quo, a united front against any perceived heresy that just might destabilise their respective positions. Even so, from a scientific point of view, there is a measure of sense in this, because even a glance at the complexity and diversity of the cosmos indicates a measure of order, logic and structure in its layout.

It is even possible to see certain universal constants here, irrespective of where they are, certain inescapable mathematical laws that seem to govern the shape and form of the constellations and galaxies. Laws that apply equally from the cosmos to the way in which architects design buildings and artists proportion paintings. It is in the shape of seashells and acorns, an ear of corn and now, evidently, in the shape of the subatomic particles that comprise the fabric of reality. Why do these unmistakable rules apply and who or what designed them that way? This measurement/ratio is called 'The Golden Section' or 'The Golden Mean' and its value is 1:1.618033988. It is exact and it is ubiquitous and has been recognised since the earliest times and humanity is still finding further examples of it in everything from the immense to the tiniest levels of existence.

Scientifically-inclined religionists, while maintaining a discreet silence on the baseless and distorted cant of the Creationists, recognise that this ratio exists in all things, but find it easier to attribute it to the design of a Creator God. Religionists, who regard scripture as revealed truth, instinctively see this as the work of an Almighty God, while other, less credulous individuals might interpret these signs as the work of some ancient civilisation that left its calling card in the form of mathematical truths, the only true form of Esperanto that might serve as a cosmic Rosetta Stone, linking the human race with its progenitors. Might these be the very beings contacted by the psychics and mediums who are frequently castigated by orthodoxy? One important school of esoteric thought, the Pythagoreans who we shall encounter again as we progress, teach that 'All is number'. In addition, as we have already mentioned, the appearance of the ratios displayed in the cosmos, in the swirls and curves of galaxies, are represented here on Earth in tiny, natural objects. This gave rise to the gnostic and magickal mantra of 'As above so below', which is another undeniable truth that will appear several times in this work.

The concept was enshrined by our forbears in the structures they built that conformed to everything from the anthromorphisation of constellations to the rising and setting of the Sun and Moon. It was true millennia ago and it is still true today and the idea is also found in Masonic teachings when they refer to, 'The Grand Geometrician of The Universe'. This is as clear a reference as one can come to admitting that the cosmos resembles a mathematical equation. Not surprisingly, 'As above as below' is also found in prayers, but, in this case, it is altered to 'In Heaven as it is on Earth' and it means exactly the same thing and for exactly the same reasons, although these tend to become altered to suit the context.

Chapter 5
The 'Big Bang' and Other Magickal Events

Let's very briefly look at something fundamental to the human condition on one level and the entire cosmos on another: the creation of the universe. According to the precepts of the 'Big Bang' theory (which, incidentally, was the brainchild of a Jesuit scientist/priest named le Maitre) the universe suddenly exploded into existence from a microscopic singularity somewhere in the order of 37 billion years ago. The solar system in which we live is around 5.5 billion years old. The development of the human race can, in various forms, be traced back for many millions of years and modern humanity in tens of thousands. This does create something of a paradox; if the cosmos was created by fiat (i.e. by command) then someone or something had to deliberately bring this act about.

The excellent communicator and populariser of physics, Professor Michio Kaku, put it this way. When Professor Kaku was young, he attended Sunday school, in spite of the fact that his parents were from a Buddhist tradition, which, of course, does not follow deist beliefs at all, and, during one lesson on scripture, he asked the teacher a simple question. The class was studying Genesis and he asked his teacher if God had a mother, the kind of simple, direct, logical and legitimate question that a child would ask. The teacher could not answer right away, except to say "probably not", but she would seek advice from the minister. What the eventual outcome was, we do not discover, because Professor Kaku, presumably, did not receive a reply. At least there is none quoted in his excellent book, Parallel Worlds. The standard answer is, of course, that God is eternal, omnipotent and omnipresent. He created the universe for His own inscrutable purposes, a position that is impregnable and unassailable, because to believe this unquestioningly is an act of faith alone and, therefore, requires neither proof nor justification. As a comment on Professor Kaku's parents, it speaks volumes for them that they were prepared to allow their son to attend a Christian children's gathering. It is unlikely that any parents of the three monotheistic faiths would allow their children such a similar freedom.

It is around such simple, yet fiendishly difficult, questions that the three main faiths revolve. Questions such as, "Is God sentient in any meaningful sense?" or "If God created the cosmos out of nothing, then who created God?" Outside of unthinking acceptance, there is no easy answer to this and it is even possible that the human race created God through necessity, because it simply did not have the ability to comprehend the deep and profound mysteries of the cosmos and their place in it. In other words, God was brought into being through a mixture of sheer necessity, fear, curiosity and innocence. The chicken or the egg writ large, indeed. One gets the uncomfortable feeling that if any one of the many huge foundation stones of faith were prized out of the edifice of religion, then the whole lot would crash around the ears of the believers.

For example, when the Jewish religion was in its infancy, it regarded Yahweh as all-conquering and all-powerful, much as Christians regard their own deity, which is, of course, the same God, since Christianity is a Jewish offshoot. During their travails, the Hebrew people were sorely tested many times and their God did not save them. However, rather than admitting this was a sign of weakness on the part of their God, they interpreted it as a demonstration of unimaginable strength that He trusted His people to rebuild and reinvent themselves. An even worse situation arose prior to and during the Second World War when the Nazis persecuted, tortured and murdered millions of Jews in the name of racial purity.

Their God did not save them, although it has been argued that His help came in the form of the Allied armies who were drawn into the conflict for a variety of reasons, either political or for self-preservation and with little thought for religion. In addition to this, God's will was seen as a significant factor in the subsequent establishment of the state of Israel. This is something that totally ignores the incessant lobbying of various governments, particularly that of Britain, by powerful and extremely wealthy Jewish families, particularly the Rothschilds, whose banking empire had repeatedly part-financed the British government in some of its expansionist ventures. An identical type of perverse logic has been shown many times both before and since when sundry doomsday cults have predicted the end of the world, only to see their predicted catastrophe come and go with the planet still intact. Nevertheless, they still predict the apocalypse with what borders on fanatical glee, knowing that they will be the only ones saved. The next Doomsday/End Times event forecast will happen on December the 21st, 2012. We will wait and see.

Mediums, Magick and the Big Bang
From the very outset, we should be aware that the very idea of communication with the deceased is regarded as utterly impossible by respectable science and, by that yardstick, it is very much the province of charlatans and the deluded. Anything that occurs which is not capable of being measured and evaluated on demand (and the keywords here are 'on demand') on anything other than a physical level is a complete anathema in scientific terms. As far as science is concerned, as we have already seen, anything with the taint of the paranormal about it is impossible and unprovable and correspondingly rejected. In spite of many serious discussions and heated exchanges among psi researchers, there is very little real consensus and perhaps part of the

problem is due to the simple lack of an acceptable common vocabulary to convey the information.

Yes, there is a lexicon of sorts relating to the subject that has percolated into the mainstream via a kind of osmotic process through the influence of mediums, psychics and channellers, but it falls far short of what might be deemed as universally acceptable to all parties. This is especially true if there is any real intention of actually presenting a comprehensive, clear and lucid case for the reality of anomalous phenomena to the mainstream scientific community. It is all very well having absolute faith in the subject, but faith is in the heart of the believers only, unless, like religion, it is shared by other interested and sympathetic parties.

Returning to the matter of the Big Bang, it is entirely possible that during this unprecedented and unsurpassed cataclysm, the seeds of supernatural, paranormal and magickal phenomena were sown. Since the core of this event was a singularity that was perhaps only the size of a grain of talcum powder, then it is reasonable to assume that everything was as one, literally. All the hyper-compressed elements that make up the cosmos as it is now were one single, solid body and, as such, were in absolute harmony and cohesion, until, in a fraction of a second, this particle was riven asunder and all its component parts were thrust out to create the cosmos and all the evidence suggests that it is still expanding after billions of years. Prior to this, there had been no time, no space and no cosmos. There was absolutely nothing, which is a difficult concept to accept: the immensity of the universe consisted of one, solitary, miniscule particle. It follows, then, that even although this singularity had been ripped and blown apart, all of the cosmos had been in contact at one point in time and that hypothesis still holds good today.

The atoms that make up every living thing on this planet still contain the core memory of oneness within that singularity therefore it should come as no surprise that these elements may still be able to communicate through one method or another. That being the case, then those who have passed over have merely divested themselves of their physical bodies while their consciousness has continued at another level, a level that, theoretically, should still be accessible. Sir James Fraser, the author of The Golden Bough, refers to this as the way in which magick functions decades before the concept of the Big Bang ever occurred to anyone. According to Sir James, magick functioned through 'sympathy', in other words, because everything in the cosmos, whether enormous or tiny, was interlinked through 'invisible connections'. It seems that certain possibilities regarding how magick operates have been in existence for a very long time indeed. It is something that is suggested by Aleister Crowley and his magickal system, but that appears a little later.

Is The End Nigh?

Here we have the sheer arrogance displayed by some elements of humanity promoting its supposedly vastly superior knowledge based on assumptions gained by interpreting sections of the Bible, usually from the obscure apocryphal books written over a vanishingly small space of time, to tell us what is true and what is false. Why would works, some of which are based on accounts of events alleged to have begun just over three thousand years ago, the Pentateuch for example, have any relevance in the great scheme of things? Having said that, as we have seen, it is also true to say that many times in the comparatively recent past, when so-called 'prophets' and 'new messiahs' have declared that some cataclysmic event would occur, such as the end of the world, and this did not occur, they still kept at least some of their credulous flock. What this seems to indicate is that the followers may be socially inadequate or the self-styled 'prophets' are extremely controlling and charismatic and have indoctrinated their followers so deeply that they are incapable of making their own decisions, or a combination of both.

The first of the monotheistic faiths, Judaism, came into existence just over 3,000 years ago and the last one, Islam, around 1,500 years ago. Christianity itself is a shade over 2,000 years old and was founded by a Jewish heretic. In other words, these dogmatic and largely intransigent belief systems have been around for almost literally less than the blink of an eye in cosmological terms. Yet, in spite of this, they preach absolute certainties based on little more than hypothesis and wishful thinking. As 'proof' of what they say, copies of various ancient documents, the Torah, the Bible and the Qur'an are produced. These, they say, are all the 'proof' that is required, because they are the revealed word of God. Unfortunately, all of these books were written by men with separate agendas to pursue and all of them depend, depict and rely, to a large extent, on supernatural beings and magickal events.

Perhaps we should pause for a moment before continuing to consider one point regarding the nature of spirituality and belief. In the course of the development of religion, in this case the Christian faith, there were those who considered the idea of a physical manifestation of God as wholly unacceptable. They were the believers in dualism who thought, and with some justification, that since the concept of a supernatural being would be something of pure spirit, the idea that the offspring of such an entity should be physical (and therefore impure) made no sense at all. Chief among these groups (and there were several) were the Cathari (from the Greek katharoi meaning pure), later to be grouped under the generic term 'The Cathars'. The reason that the Catholic Church was, and still is, set against dualistic practices stems from the biblical injunction that God created the world and, to quote from scripture, 'Saw that it was good'.

The Cathars considered, in line with Islam, that any physical representation of God, as exhibited in churches and possessions, was evil and only the spiritual aspect could be the way to salvation. The authorities, in the form of the Catholic Church, would have none of this, since it profoundly affected both the way in which it was financed and the sumptuous lifestyles of many of those who governed it. At first, the Church attempted to convince these heretics that they were wrong, but, unfortunately, some of the emissaries sent to reason with the Cathars started to see the attraction and logic of the Cathars dualistic faith and joined them. As we will see later, it was the much-maligned Cathari who, indirectly, were responsible for the founding of the Dominican order of monks. The upshot of this display of perceived heresy was the Albigensian Crusade and the consequent murder of tens of thousands in the name of conformity. Fortunately, in our comparatively enlightened times, there is little fear of death and retribution for those who choose to follow their own beliefs, except in the case of Islam, where apostasy (denying the faith or, worse still, converting to another) is still punishable by summary execution.

Chapter 6
The Witches and The Alchemists

There are two very clear examples illustrating the frequently schizophrenic attitude of the Church authorities to magick and these are the apparent contradictions in how witchcraft and alchemy were dealt with. This, mark you, is without going into how medieval scientists were viewed when their factual evidence contradicted that of Church dogma, which was based largely on conjecture and various interpretations of scripture. Having said that, scientists and alchemists were often regarded as one and the same thing anyway.

The Witches
The very word, 'witch', conjures up a myriad of images in the mind's eye and none of them necessarily edifying. These impressions have resulted from centuries of fear and ignorance assiduously encouraged and cheered on by a largely hostile and scandalised establishment, usually in the form of the established Christian Church. It is even formalised in the Bible under the stern exhortation, 'Thou shalt not suffer a witch to live' [Exodus 22:18], although sometimes the word used for witch translates as 'sorceress'. As we will see, this apparently unambiguous comment was used to great and tragic effect during the notorious persecution of witches that occurred in the Middle Ages. Such was the degree of gullibility and fear, any propaganda put out by the authorities, no matter how ridiculous, was accepted by the largely uneducated and superstitious masses without demur. Sadly, many Christian fundamentalist groups still adhere to this biblical pronouncement in thought if not in deed.

Perhaps we should pause briefly to look at this contentious line from Exodus in a little more detail. In the original Hebrew the text reads: 'M'khashephah lo tichayyah', which means, 'May a m'khashephah not live' or 'You will not keep a m'khashephah in life'. M'khashephah is the feminine form of m'khasheph, which is the masculine. It means someone who practiced 'k'shaphim', a variety of magick which used supernatural forces to cause changes in the environment. This, quite conveniently, was a charge frequently laid at the door of many alleged witches. The proscription of witchcraft as a purely female manifestation is also found in an ancient Irish poem attributed to Saint Patrick called The Deer's Cry. In the poem, the person begs to be protected from 'briochta ban' or 'women's spells', among other forms of harmful magick. As we shall see, this feminisation of those capable of causing harm though magick is absolutely typical of the baleful misogyny and hypocrisy displayed by the Roman Catholic Church during the Dark and Middle Ages.

The origins of witchcraft are as old as mankind itself. It is almost certain that it grew from the remnants of ancient, nature-based folk religions and beliefs. Traces of early witchcraft can be found in early Egyptian writings, describing magicians and fortune-tellers who drew their powers from unearthly beings and devils. However, it is likely that there was some confusion between genuine mystics and what we would now term as entertainers and conjurers. It is also true that the translation of the Hebrew word for a witch, M'khashephah, in the King James-sponsored translation of the Bible in 1611, would carry a completely different interpretation than would be put on it now. Stories of this type are also found in the records of ancient Greece and Rome. Indeed, it was the Roman emperor, Valerian, who instigated the first witchhunts as we would understand the term.

From these early and fragmented beginnings, it gradually coalesced into animistic worship of natural forces, be they deemed physical or spiritual. Although the early Christian Church of the 4th and 5th Centuries disapproved of this form of worship, it was, at that time, neither particularly widespread nor powerful. Therefore, since it was in no position to actively attack any pagan faith, it was, for the most part, pragmatic and co-existed with the old religions and beliefs. Indeed, it was not uncommon for early Christian priests to participate in ceremonies glorifying these older and, perhaps, much more satisfying faiths.

In order to bring as many people within the tenets of its teaching as possible, the ever-practical early Church announced that, in order for the followers of these ancient religions to join the growing band of Christian believers, all they had to do was publicly renounce their old ways. It was not until approximately 1050AD, by which time the Christian Church had absorbed most of the adherents of the by now rapidly disintegrating early beliefs, that the desire to hunt down and destroy the remaining practitioners of the old religions began to take hold in Europe. As we have already seen, the official justification for this was the biblical command, "Thou shalt not permit a sorceress/witch to live."

The Alchemists

The process and discipline of alchemy has been expressed in various forms. On one level, it is regarded as a quest for spiritual perfection and on another as a scientific process with quasi-magickal overtones designed to convert base metals into gold. Unlike witchcraft, whose roots of nature worship thread back for millennia, the practice of alchemy (a word with Arabic origins) can be dated back to around 300BC and, like witchcraft, had never enjoyed a favourable image with either the laity or, latterly, the Church. This was due to what was seen as meddling with the forces of nature and invoking demons and elemental forces, which was especially true when the alchemists began to challenge the highly simplistic, accepted wisdom that the natural world was composed of only four elements: earth, air, fire and water. Although alchemy had begun with straightforward, practical experimentation, by the 4th Century AD, due to their lack of success, the introduction of rather more esoteric methods was instituted. These methods included incantations, astrology, magick and ritual and many of the ingredients used in attempts to produce the elusive 'Philosophers' Stone' were, to say the least, bizarre.

Before continuing, it may be informative to examine the role of the Islamic world in the development of alchemy. The word itself comes from the Arabic 'Al-Kimia' or 'the Kimia', along with other associated words such as 'chemist' and 'chemical' and alcohol (which came via the French language, but, once again, originated from the Arabic, 'Al-Khul' or 'the Khul') and, indeed, so did the word alkali, or 'the Kali'. Although Islam did not emerge until approx 500AD, it is significant that Islamic scholars and scientists contributed so much to the lexicon of both alchemy and to chemistry in general. There is a good reason for this, although, as we have already mentioned, the idea of converting base metal to gold originated with the pre-Christian mystery schools, it was the Catholic Church, although grudgingly tolerant of alchemy, that actively discouraged scientific experimentation, especially anything that ran contrary to its own heavily blinkered dogma. It was this stifling set of inflexible rules that held back the development of real science in the west all through the Dark and Middle Ages.

This was a self-limiting outlook that slowly changed with the continuing spread of Islam, whose still-emerging rules did not, at that time, specifically forbid wide-ranging and adventurous exploration into the processes governing the physical world. This perceived freedom of expression was one of the many drivers behind the ferocious and ruinously expensive series of crusades launched against Islam. It may also come as a surprise that it was Islamic chemists (al-chemists) who are credited with discovering the process of distilling and producing alcohol and saw no dichotomy in using alcohol (the consumption of which is, of course, anathema in Islam) as part of their experimentation.

All manner of items and ingredients were used in the experiments, various raw chemicals, human blood and sperm, even parts of aborted foetuses, anything that these early chemists had decided would produce the miraculous catalyst needed to bring about the mystical and physical change. The quest for the mysterious catalyst involved invoking the 'life force', which was assumed to be at the core of everything and, therefore, possessed great power, hence the use of blood and sperm, both items that found similar uses in magickal ceremonies, but more of that later. These men were truly operating at the absolute cutting edge of their technology, literally treading on unknown and quite terrifying ground. Although their antics would presumably have introduced a certain degree of theatricality to the proceedings, it is reasonably safe to assume that no gold was ever actually produced. Any claims that gold was actually manufactured using these processes must be viewed with great suspicion, although, predictably, some supposedly was. Despite that, what was produced were some of the earliest examples of amalgams and alloys of metals. Incidentally, if gold actually was produced, then the secret and process conveniently vanished along with its unknown inventor.

The introduction of these methods is surprising, given that certain leading churchmen, most notably the English monk, Roger Bacon, were responsible for considerable detailed and practical research into the subject. This type of double standard is found when one looks at the allied subjects of Satanism and magick of the blackest kind, because semi-magickal/religious incantations of various sorts were used during alchemical operations. Added to this, none other than the 13th Century Pope Honorius III himself compiled what is widely regarded as the most dangerous book of spells and incantations ever assembled, The Grimoire of Pope Honorius III.

Perhaps he justified this opus, which frequently involved human sacrifice to operate the spells, on the grounds that it gave him a better understanding of the evils that surround us and, as such, serve as a kind of spiritual armour, perhaps... or perhaps it was designed for a much more sinister purpose. It may even have acted as a kind of 'belt and braces' approach in terms of exerting control. If God could not help, then perhaps his implacable foe could. That said, the collection of spells and invocations in the volume include several verses designed to invoke the protection of God and/or His angels on the person using it, but it is difficult to see how anyone professing faith, especially the Vicar of Christ, could rationalise this. In addition, there are some parts of the grimoire that can only be conducted by an ordained priest and involve, among other things, animal mutilation.

Sympathetic Magick and the Church

That aside, the probable reason for the exclusion of alchemists during the fervour of the witchhunts was due to the fact that they were operating with some degree of either royal or church patronage and protection. Perhaps greed would be the obvious reason for the transmutation of base metals into gold via the medium of the so-called Philosophers' Stone. Any method by which this feat could be achieved would have ensured protection from the zealots and, if successful, an excellent source of revenue for royal and/or Church coffers, both organisations being continually strapped for cash to fund their various projects. Prior to the tantalising possibility of riches being gained through the conversion of base metals to gold, the Church and state had used the time honoured methods of taxation and, in the case of the Catholic Church, the sale of indulgences and supposed holy relics etc. The latter two sources of income were curious practices whereby members of the clergy, from the Pope down, offered their flock (A) expiation from sin by literally buying salvation with cash or goods and (B) the sale of shrivelled body parts, supposedly belonging to dead saints etc.

The second lucrative (and rather grizzly) practice sometimes resulted in shortages of appropriate parts, so the corpses of better-known saints apparently donated a remarkable number of fingers, toes and other appendages to the trade. So short did the parts become that is was not uncommon for various diocese to pool their recourses to buy one relic to share between them on a rota basis. The sale of the body parts of the crucified Christ did not occur simply because He was taken bodily to Heaven by the Father on the third day after His death. There was, however, a market for relics that were taken before His death, including clothing and hair clippings, and we must not forget His prepuce (foreskin), which was removed at His circumcision. The Catholic Church still venerates this artefact on the 1st of January during the 'Feast of the Circumcision' and as recently as 1983 it was actually exhibited in its jewel-encrusted reliquary during a procession in the Italian village of Calcata. Unfortunately, thieves stole both the reliquary and its contents and, so far, it has not reappeared. There was one interesting story surrounding this item where one 17th Century theologian, Leo Allatius, stated that the foreskin had also ascended to Heaven upon the death of Christ, where it had become the rings around Saturn.

The other thing that is highly relevant about the use of relics in a display of transferred magick is their supposed power to heal the sick by touch and stop droughts and all manner of other natural occurrences. This function is precisely the same as the use of sympathetic magick to heal and is remarkably similar to the alleged ability of royalty, both English and French, to use this supposed gift to heal the disfiguring disease, scrofula, which is a type of tuberculosis. The Merovingians were one such royal house reputed to heal the sick by touch, along with a succession of English and French kings. King Henry IV of France was particularly noted for this ability and the practice continued until the 18th Century. The gift came from the so-called 'Divine Right of Kings', where the position of kingship was given direct from God and, therefore, the king was answerable to God and God alone. This unique position finds resonance in the belief in 'Papal Infallibility', where any pronouncement made by the Pope in regard to Catholic dogma is presumed to be absolutely correct.

There is another curious fact relating to the use of relics and that was something called 'furta sacra' or 'pious theft', when various odds and ends, supposedly from saints, were 'translated' from one place to another or, in plain language, stolen. We have to keep in mind that these relics were regarded as the saints themselves in the flesh and if any relic was in a particular town or city then the saint that it came from was actually there too.

This, therefore, was taken to mean that the saint was being kidnapped with his or her approval, because if the saint did not approve of the removal then, quite naturally, the translation/theft could not take place, because spiritual forces would prevent it. Fortunately, all the clandestine 'translations' must have been approved of, or at the very least condoned, since there are no recorded instances of any spiritual minders appearing to foil the thefts.

Chapter 7
The Inquisition and the Suppression of Heresy

Even with the instinctive antipathy towards non-standard beliefs, there was a certain degree of tolerance of witchcraft that continued for centuries, until, in the year 1448, Pope Innocent VIII issued the key Papal bull directed against witchcraft, the 'Summis Desiderantes Affectibus' or 'Wishing with the Greatest Concern'. To implement this, he appointed inquisitors for each region to ensure that his instructions were carried out. It is important to remember that, by 15th Century, witches were no longer seen as eccentric dispensers of natural cures, rather, thanks to relentless propagandising by the Church, the term 'witch' had become synonymous with Satanic worship, a lie still prevalent today.

It was not true then and it is not true now. Witchcraft, Wicca and Satanism are not necessarily connected. Modern witches reject the very idea of Satanic involvement and the celebration of the 'Black Mass', preferring to point out that they practice magick and worship elder gods, but not Satan. Occasionally, the practice of Voodoo (and its variants) is incorporated into the wider picture of witchcraft, which totally ignores the fact that Voodoo is a hybrid of Christianity and traditional African beliefs. Voodoo ceremonies and rites are designed to protect the practitioner against witchcraft and other perceived supernatural wickedness. It is even arguable that Voodoo is gnostic in its approach, since it involves its participants in achieving trance-like states to achieve personal union with its gods and we shall return to the subject of gnostic belief in more detail a little later.

The Papal bull served to justify the creation of a document entitled The Malleus Maleficarum or Hammer of the Witches, written by two Dominican monks (or perhaps that should be superstitious, pious psychopaths), Heinrich Insitoris and Jakob Sprenger and published in 1486, although sometimes the name, Insitoris, is replaced by another Dominican, Kramer. Indeed, to increase its authority, the document even incorporated the Papal bull in the introduction. This distasteful manuscript described in great detail how punishments should be meted out and how to frame the incriminating questions so that anyone accused of witchcraft would be hard put to avoid incriminating themselves. It clearly stated that no mercy should be shown to suspects and the 'truth' obtained by application of the prescribed tortures should be taken as valid. It should be pointed out that Sprenger later renounced the work and Insitoris with it and Insitoris, himself, was eventually condemned by his own monastic order for embezzlement and corruption.

This notwithstanding, he remained active in witchhunting until the end of the century.

We should be clear that there were at least two Inquisitions, the Medieval Inquisition, created and enforced by the Papacy, and the slightly later Spanish Inquisition, invoked in the 15th Century by King Ferdinand II of Aragon and Queen Isabella I of Castile. Although the Inquisitions had different originators, their purpose was basically the same, suppressing heresy and enforcing rigid control over the population, and both were carried out with an astonishing degree of single-minded and vicious zealotry. It is arguable that this shocking period in history was one of the first large scale attempts at mind control through the use of terror, psychological manipulation and physical torture. The fact that the belongings of those who were put to 'the question' (i.e. into the hands of the torturers) and, almost invariably, found guilty were forfeit and added to the coffers of either the Church or the State, did little to discourage its horrific excesses. In most cases, it did not matter anyway, because, in effect, the Church and State was one and the same thing.

The virtually inevitable confessions of guilt were always extracted by the application of the vilest tortures imaginable and because the Church was involved, the idea was that no blood should be shed. This led to the use of the 'boot' to crush limbs to a pulp, the 'strappado' to dislocate the arms at the shoulder joints, the rack for a similar purpose and tearing off gobbets of flesh with red-hot pincers and often a combination of these methods. This last technique mentioned did not actually spill blood because the heat from the pincers cauterised the wounds as the flesh was ripped off. It is known that the pitiful victims of this hellish process often had to drag themselves to the stake because of the damage inflicted on them and frequently they (or their families) were forced to pay for the services of the executioner and the wood used to burn them. Incidentally, the torture was often a two-stage process where, once 'the question' had been answered in a manner suitable to the inquisitor, further 'persuasion' was used to elicit the names of other heretics and these were inevitably forthcoming. Truly, if Satan walked the Earth in these dark days, it was in the guise of the merciful God who apparently heartily approved of this church-instigated brutality.

The initial question was, "Do you believe in witchcraft?" A straightforward question, or so it seems, but there was no way out of this horrible situation. To answer 'no' was a serious heresy because the Church obviously did believe, so, therefore, a negative reply denied the Church's teaching and might result in death anyway. To answer 'yes', although complying with Church doctrine, was obviously at least part way to an admission of guilt and opened the door to series of thirty-two loaded questions and failure to answer any one of them was regarded as a sure sign of guilt. Each admission to a specific question also allowed the inquisitor to further tease out a more elaborate and damning 'confession'.

The questions consisted of items like:

How long have you been a witch?
Why did you become a witch?
Who was the one you chose to be your incubus and what was
his name?
What was the name of your master among the evil demons?
What was the oath you were forced to render to him?
How did you make this oath and what were its conditions?
Which finger were you forced to raise?
Where did you consummate your union with your incubus?
What demons and what other humans participate at the sabbat?

All utter nonsense, but on and on it went and the penalties attached to the forgone conclusion of guilt were as follows: For those who practice the invocation of evil spirits, for any purpose, the punishment is death. Those who practice witchcraft and sorceries for the divination of treasure trove, the recovery of lost property, murder, bodily injury, intent to cause the two previous and destruction of goods, destruction of goods and livestock, unlawful love, destruction of the cross and the theft of corpses.

All of those were capital offences with the addition of the confiscation of property. How these inquisitors, these men who worshipped and served a supposedly loving God, could have done this in the name of their compassionate and merciful master is beyond the understanding of any rational human being. But these individuals were not rational, they were profoundly superstitious, ideological zealots, absolutely convinced of their own officially-sanctioned rightness. Their actions can be directly compared to the gut-wrenching cruelty and brutality meted out by the Nazis in the death camps and the oppressive and vicious regimes in any totalitarian society whether ancient or modern.

Chapter 8
The Monastic Orders and the Medieval Inquisition

There were two organisations charged with seeking out and eliminating heresy in the Medieval Inquisition, the Franciscan and Dominican orders of monks, although it was the Dominicans who seem to have been the most zealous, one might even say obsessive, in their duties. This particular order of monks was founded by Dominic de Guzman, who was one of the especially pious individuals elevated to sainthood by the Catholic Church, for the express purpose of uprooting perceived heresies such as the dualistic and gnostic ideas promoted by the unfortunate, previously mentioned Cathars. Typical of his ilk, Dominic was noted for eating the poorest food available, dressing in virtual rags, walking barefoot over rocky ground and any other method of self-abasement to help demonstrate the strength of his beliefs. It is worth pointing out that many of those who are now venerated as saints, especially those from the early days of the Church, would, in modern times, probably be diagnosed as either insane or, at least, in need of professional psychiatric treatment. I suggested this to an open-minded Jesuit priest during the research carried out while writing this book and, to my surprise, he was, broadly speaking, in agreement. St Dominic was no different and the legends start from just before he was born.

The practice of mortification of the flesh can, in one form or another, be found in various religions and is regularly used by the sadhus or holy men of Hinduism, it is also practiced to this day by the Roman Catholic organisation, Opus Dei, some of whose members regularly wear and/or use devices designed to produce physical discomfort. One such is 'the cilice', which is a wrap made of spiked wire designed to be worn under clothing around the arm or leg. There is also 'the discipline', which is a type of whip use to strike the skin on the back. In addition, there are also other non-approved articles used, such as wearing the equivalent of a hair shirt. In the case of Opus Dei, these practices are apparently intended to emulate (or empathise with) the suffering of Christ on the cross. One factor usually overlooked in the process of self-mortification is the fact that, in extreme cases of asceticism, the human brain can and does produce neurotransmitters, natural hallucinogens like serotonin, designed to alter consciousness and alleviate the pain and distress resulting from the self-inflicted ordeal. There is also the likelihood that other brain chemicals that can produce feelings of ecstasy and pleasure, like endorphins, are released. These natural chemicals, and others like them, produce visions and other types of altered and elevated states of awareness. Although these glimpses of an 'otherworld' may have some legitimacy, it is a type of natural defence mechanism that could easily be deemed as magickal, but this kind of magick is, presumably, quite acceptable and approved of by the Church, because it serves to prove its case.

According to a probably apocryphal legend, prior to giving birth to Dominic, his mother had a dream where a dog leaped from her womb with a lit torch grasped in its mouth and set fire to the Earth. The story did not emerge till after the founding of the Dominican order, which was named after him and, in Latin, Dominican becomes Dominicus, which can be interpreted as Domini canis or 'the Lord's hound'. A modern variant of this can be seen in the former Cardinal Joseph Ratzinger, who is the current Pope Benedict XIV, and was nicknamed 'God's Rottweiler', based upon his enthusiasm for the organisation that he once headed, the 'Congregation for the Doctrine of the Faith', the modern name for the old Inquisition. Might this be history repeating itself, because Pope Benedict is notoriously conservative in his outlook? Although Benedict's instinctive conservatism is widely acknowledged, it has been speculated that the Curia (or Vatican government) is even more so and is at great pains to preserve the public face of the Vatican as something beyond reproach. Correspondingly, there is every chance that it has been responsible for suppressing any scandals that might have affected the public perception of the institution as beyond reproach. In other words, the Curia may have exerted pressure on the Pope to carry out its wishes rather than the other way round.

In 1203, St Dominic accompanied Diego de Acebo, the Bishop of Osma, on a journey over the Pyrenees and encountered the Cathars, whose power base was in the region. It was the first time that St Dominic had encountered heresy on such a large scale and, to make matters worse, the Cathars had little or no respect for either Dominic, the bishop or indeed the Pope himself. What really surprised him was the fact that those who espoused the heretical beliefs were not ignorant and uneducated peasants, but were obviously well-informed and educated men, especially the 'Perfecti', who were those who had attained a remarkable degree of spiritual purity. While he obviously thoroughly disapproved of and abhorred the Cathar philosophy, he was intelligent enough to realise that a convincing and demonstrable argument would be needed to defeat such a deeply-rooted and seductive sect. To this end, he remained in the location for a number of years and, circa 1204, he opened his first monastic community, intended as a refuge for women who had lived in Cathar communities.

One of the many tales and fables surrounding the piety of Dominic concerns a discussion he had with the Cathars. In order to demonstrate whose truth was the most powerful, Dominic arranged a test, a challenge if you like, and religious books sacred to Dominic and the local Cathari community were thrown into a fire. In what has to be a clear demonstration of either magick or chicanery, the books of the Cathars were destroyed, but those of St Dominic were miraculously (magickally?) undamaged.

Following an unsuccessful attempt by representatives of the Holy See to dissuade the Cathars from their continuing heresies, which, to the horror of the Vatican, actually saw some of those sent to combat the heresy actually join the Cathar movement, in 1208, Dominic was in a position to set up his first proper monastic house. However, the extreme asceticism he imposed and his emphasis on prayer did not encourage many to join him, but, eventually, he succeeded in attracting a number of similarly-minded individuals, some might even say that they were zealots. It was at this time that one of the cornerstones in their philosophy was founded i.e. to find truth, no matter where it might be. Unfortunately, for those arraigned before the much later Inquisition, this rather depended on what version of the truth they wanted to find. However, it was not until 1217 that Pope Honorius III finally granted his permission to found the 'Ordo Praedicatorum' or 'Order of the Preachers'. Keeping in mind that this is the same Pope Honorius who created the infamous grimoire of magick and demonism, this leads to an interesting aside.

The reason that priests are often linked to magick and magickal practices is based on the premise that since priests are able, theoretically at least, to cast out and exorcise demons and invading spirits, they should be able to materialise and control them as well. Whether they can or not is another matter entirely, but it may be one of the reasons behind the desire of Honorius to compile his foul grimoire. Since the remit of the Dominicans was one of seeking spiritual truth and spreading the word of their God, it was almost inevitable that the role masterminding and controlling the Inquisition should fall to them. They did not actually administer the tortures, but stood by to ask any questions necessary and record the agonised responses while others did the work. They started with the Cathars and, after this heresy was eliminated, they spread their reign of oppression and terror to encompass the Waldensians and any other non-approved variant of Catholicism they uncovered.

The range of charges brought under the Inquisition included bigamy, blasphemy and homosexuality, including sodomy, although in 1509 this was adjudged as not being a crime unless it directly involved heresy, although it did not prevent twelve people being burned at the stake in the three years prior to this. Another area that might lead to charges of heresy was the possession of books deemed unsuitable for the laity, simply because reading them might lead to independent thought, which was something to be resisted at all costs. This led to the creation of a list of banned books, which included many works on science and led to the virtual stagnation of any meaningful scientific research in Spain and other areas of Europe. This list of banned books continued in a watered-down form until the 20th Century, when

Catholic newspapers regularly used to condemn books (and films) as 'pernicious' or 'spiritually damaging' and to be avoided. This guaranteed that some of the faithful would go out of their way to seek out the book or film in question to see what the fuss was about and, perhaps, in the process be duly appalled and/or titillated by what they saw. Also proscribed was Freemasonry, which obviously indicates that this particular secret and, by association, magickal society was in existence centuries before its official recognition in 18th Century England.

Then, of course, there is witchcraft, which was perhaps the most heinous heresy of them all. Little wonder, then, that the first witches were also Cathars. Strangely enough, at first the Inquisition regarded witchcraft as a mere superstition confined to the peasant classes and one of the inquisitors even went so far as to say that, in many villages, there was no sign of witchcraft until it was talked and written about. If all of this sounds in any way familiar, it should be no real surprise, because it is a prime example of the many vicious pogroms perpetrated against various minority groups both before and since by heavy-handed governments fearful of losing their grip on power. The Nazis under Hitler and the fearsome and oppressive communist regimes of Joseph Stalin, Pol Pot and, more recently, that of Kim Jong Il in North Korea are the most obvious, although it is very easy for any one party system to become inward-looking, fearful and nihilistic.

It is also interesting to note that, especially in the case of Kim Jong Il, there is still an ongoing and thriving attempt to elevate him to the level of a deity possessed of preternatural abilities. It is a cult of personality, pure and simple, designed to keep those unfortunate enough to actually live in North Korea in his thrall. It was once seriously suggested that when a tumour grew on his neck, rather than just say it was a tumour, the party machine created a story that the 'Dear Leader', as he is called, had grown an extra brain so that he could give more consideration to his people and their needs. The truly depressing thing is that some of his unfortunate and brainwashed subjects actually believed it. Needless to say, the 'Dear Leader' enjoys a lavish lifestyle that the impoverished citizens of that benighted country can only dream of. Recent events indicate that, in Russia, there are even attempts afoot to rehabilitate Joseph Stalin and conveniently sideline the horrendous spate of political assassinations that were organised via the regime imposed by this man and his handpicked government. It is arguable that these dictators and others like them organised what might be called a form of inquisition where those who failed to join the regime and share its ethos were cast aside as political heretics and either consigned to a life of brutal labour or just killed out of hand. One is reminded of the old saying, 'consume, be silent and die'.

The Spanish Inquisition

Of all the Inquisitions invoked in the name of God to suppress free thought, surely the one that evokes the most terror was the Spanish Inquisition, overseen by a man whose name is a byword for implacable intolerance, zealotry and cruelty, the Dominican friar and Inquisitor General of Spain, Tomas de Torquemada. He was described in glowing terms by one chronicler as 'The hammer of heretics, the light of Spain, the saviour of his country, the honour of his order'. In addition to seeking witches and magicians wherever he could find them, he also waged a brutal campaign against Jewish and Muslim converts to Catholicism and threw his considerable influence behind the 1492 Alhambra Decree, which involved the total expulsion of Jews from Spain. In the time that Torquemada was Inquisitor General, a post given to him by Queen Isabella in 1483, the number of people executed by *auto-de-fe* (burned alive at the stake) in Spain stood at around two thousand.

During the existence of the Inquisition in Spain, every Christian, i.e. Catholic, over the age of twelve for females and fourteen for males, was accountable to it, as were all those who had converted from other beliefs, perhaps especially those who had converted, because they might be practicing their former faiths in secret. In fact, anyone who held views that did not align with the state religion were automatically suspect and had to exercise special care in their words and deeds. In addition, anyone who spoke out against the bloody excesses of the Inquisition or did not make strenuous efforts to attend the public executions was, likewise, automatically suspect. Under the instructions of Torquemada, the single location of the 'Holy Office' in Seville, which oversaw the day-to-day running of Inquisition, was expanded until there were more than twenty of them throughout the country. As with the other versions of the Inquisition, burning supposedly heretical books was a popular method of suppressing dissident spiritual views, which led to any copies of the Talmud found being burned along with anything Arabic. This might seem a rather childish and petty exercise in modern times, but bear in mind that, in those days, books were extremely expensive, highly prized and few in number.

This is not to say that the actions approved and sanctioned by Torquemada went unnoticed by those in authority. Prior to the appointment of Torquemada to Chief Inquisitor, Pope Sixtus IV observed that the so-called 'Holy Office of the Inquisition' was arresting people on charges of heresy with no foundation other than rumour and hearsay, torturing them, taking their money and property and sentencing them to death. This caused some of those worried that the dead hand of the Inquisition might soon be upon their shoulders to approach the Vatican, loudly protesting their innocence and orthodoxy of belief. So hated and feared did Torquemada become that he was eventually forced to travel with a permanent bodyguard of some 300 armed guards in a mixture of cavalry and foot soldiers. It is rumoured that, rather like Adolph Hitler being the only man with nothing to fear from the abhorred head of the SS, Reichsfuerer Heinrich Himmler, the only person with some degree of immunity from Torquemada's predations was the Pope himself. Another interesting comparison between demagogues like Torquemada and Adolph Hitler, in particular, is that, in addition to being Catholic, like Hitler (and, of course, Himmler), in common with Hitler, Torquemada had Jewish ancestry. In fact, his grandmother was a Jewish convert, the very people that he instinctively distrusted.

Following his death in 1498, such was the atmosphere of secrecy surrounding the workings of the Inquisition that his manual of instruction governing its operations, the 'Copilacion de las Instruciones del Offico de la Sancta Inquisicion', was not released into the public domain until 1576 in Madrid. The sheer hatred of the man resurfaced in 1832 when his tomb was broken into, his skeleton stolen and burned to ashes. Actually, the connections between evil people like Himmler and Hitler and associations with magick go rather further than just mere circumstance. It has long been mooted in some quarters that Adolph Hitler was in league with the forces of darkness, which, given his track record, is not a difficult comparison to make, but like so many of these charges, other than what is written in books like The Spear of Destiny by Trevor Ravenscroft, the actual hard evidence is scanty. On the other hand, it is known that powerful individuals within the Nazi hierarchy, like Heinrich Himmler, were of a decidedly mystical bent and his project to rebuild Wewelsberg Castle was an example of this. It was intended as a spiritual home (if spiritual is a term that can be used in this context) for his beloved SS and an indoctrination centre to drive home his views on the ancestry and racial superiority of the German and Aryan nation. Fortunately, the end of the Third Reich came before any of this dangerous ideological and occult meddling could be brought to fruition.

Chapter 9
Gilles de Rais

Perhaps the worst instances of Satanic excess and the celebration of the Black Mass ever to emerge in Europe were the alleged atrocities surrounding a man who, at one time, was elevated to the rank of Marshal of France and had been closely associated with a great French heroine, the enigmatic and troubled Joan of Arc. This brave and intensely spiritual young woman was, herself, eventually accused of practicing witchcraft and piously murdered by the Church and State when her usefulness was perceived to be at an end. The man in question was Gilles de Rais, more correctly known as Gilles de Laval, the Lord of Rais, a courageous and astute warrior in the cause of king and country. However, his end in no way reflected his honour but, instead, his inexorable slide into Satanism, paedophilia, debauchery and eventual perdition. Gilles was born of minor royalty in Machecoul, France, in 1404 and his upbringing, although he showed a precocious intelligence, was relatively unremarkable. Until at the age of sixteen, he served in the army during the War of the Breton Succession, where, as a Breton knight, his acts of bravery and leadership caught the attention of his superiors, who introduced him to court life. In 1427, aged only twenty-three, he was elevated to the rank of commander in the French army and successfully supported Joan of Arc during the Hundred Years War and was present with Joan when the Siege of Orleans came to an end. For his devoted service, he was awarded the prestigious rank of Marshal of France at the consecration of Charles VII as King of France.

Although he had served with Joan, 'The Maid of Orleans', he was absent at her execution when, in May, 1431, she was burned at the stake and he was not seen to take any part in her defence. Perhaps brutalised by his earlier experiences on the battlefield, the first signs of his sociopathic and psychopathic tendencies began to surface and he began indulging his violent tastes through raids on local farmers and seizing wealthy merchants for ransom. The proceeds of these criminal endeavours partly financed his extravagant lifestyle and almost incredibly his simultaneous patronage of the arts and church. At around this time, his grandfather, who had, to a large part, created the wealth that Gilles had come to rely on, died and, in a clear sign of his disapproval at his grandson's spendthrift ways and destruction of the carefully husbanded fortune, left his sword and breastplate to Gilles' younger brother, René. It may seem a minor issue to the modern reader, but at that time, it was regarded as a major slight and insult.

Shortly after this, Gilles (who also found lasting fame as 'Bluebeard') began to forsake his public and army duties, preferring instead to concentrate on his own pursuits and commenced on two ruinously expensive projects. One was the construction of the 'Chapel of the Holy Innocents' and the other was an elaborate piece of theatre based on his successful earlier military exploits called Le Mistère du Siège d'Orléans. These two vanity projects almost bankrupted him, forcing him to sell off some of his estates to pay the rapidly escalating bills. By 1432, his family, perhaps fearing for their own inheritances, tried to stop his lavish spending. They first appealed to Pope Eugene IV to exert some influence by severing any connection with the Chapel of the Holy Innocents, but the Pope refused to do this, because it did not suit his own agenda, so the family then approached the king. Here they had more success and, in 1435, the king issued instructions to the towns and villages close to Gilles' estates that no business of any kind was to be transacted with him and that he, specifically, was forbidden to trade with them.

According to the testimony given at his later trial, it was at this point he seems to have begun his gradual slide into irredeemable evil. Perhaps the indicators were already there, but masked behind his apparent acts of extravagance and philanthrophy or perhaps they had already been evident in the bloody savagery and brutality of his battlefield actions. That said, the battles in those days were a far cry from the semi-clinical actions seen today. These fights were literally up close and personal with no quarter given on either side, so perhaps any excessive or gratuitous brutality was difficult to detect. According to the trial documents, de Rais fell under the thrall of a man called Francesco Prelati, some kind of alchemist/sorcerer who supposedly promised that his fortunes would be restored through magickal means by sacrificing children to a demon called 'Barron'.

We have to be careful here, because in order to make sense of the appalling carnage that followed, with hindsight it may have been necessary to construct a feasible explanation to justify it. According to what evidence there is, the murders began circa 1432 and continued for several years after and the number of bodies found on his properties varies wildly between forty and six hundred, although it is beyond doubt that the bodies of badly mutilated children were found. It is also beyond doubt that they were sacrificed in a series of horrific rituals and offered up to whatever demonic entity de Rais tried to invoke. I should caution the reader that I have no intention of going into any great detail concerning what was done to those these poor children, save to say that it greatly surpasses anything that has been revealed to date in lurid tabloid newspaper accounts regarding any child abuse scandals. The foul rituals involved pederasty and necrophilia and if anyone feels the need to read all the particularly nasty and sickening details of these events there are ample resources that will allow them to do so.

As far as I am concerned, they are profoundly troubling and only serve to demonstrate just how far human beings are willing to degrade and debase themselves and, as a result, humanity itself, in their pursuit of influence and gratification. The desire to command magickal powers does not require anything like that. The truly astonishing thing is that, prior to his execution, de Rais appealed for forgiveness, saying, "You who are present, you above all, whose children I have slain, I am your brother in Christ. By Our Lord's Passion, I implore you, pray for me. Forgive me with all your hearts the evil I have done you, as you yourselves hope for God's mercy and pardon." This is, indeed, a moving request and contemporary accounts reveal that there were those who wept copiously for him as the fire was lit, so, what to make of it? Was this an impassioned speech of the most appallingly hypocritical and mawkish kind or were these the final words of a truly repentant soul?

Is it possible that de Rais was genuinely possessed of some kind of invading demon and totally unaware of what he had done or was he suffering from a psychiatric condition like schizophrenia or split personality (there are ample case histories to support this hypothesis) or was a rabid sociopath and serial killer attempting to gain access to a dark power? Sociopathic tendencies, if that was what they were, would have made him incapable of regarding that what he was doing was in any way wrong or inappropriate, let alone the epitome of evil. Two of these possibilities are valid and could allow him to genuinely repent for what he had done. After all, he never denied that he and his accomplices had carried out these foul actions. According to the teachings of the Catholic Church (and Gilles de Rais was a devout Catholic), an invading demon can and will take over all the functions of a human being who, outwardly at least, would give no sign of possession, unless, of course, the demon wanted to. These normally consist of displays of incredible strength, the ability to speak a foreign language that should be unknown to the possessed person, the ability to foretell the future and abilities of that type. These were never noted with de Rais.

Even if he was possessed, how would this have happened? Was it because of the foul ceremonies and rites in which he took part or was he somehow 'opened up' and 'pre-primed' during the slaughter of the battlefield years earlier? If he had been genuinely possessed and the demon had been removed or, in the face of the imminent death of its host, gone of its own accord, then he would, indeed, have been horrified at what he had done under its influence. If, on the other hand, he had been mentally ill, then there might well have been spells of remission, but, if so, then they would surely have occurred spontaneously during his rampage and given him cause to stop. These possibilities are all valid and it is fortunate for de Rais, exalted position or not, that the Inquisition was not in force during his reign of terror. Whatever, it is abundantly clear that the Christ he so eloquently invokes was sadly absent during the sexual abuse, torture and murder of these innocents. The last word on this particularly repellent series of events comes from something that occurred as the remains of de Rais hung smouldering from the stake: a large black fly was seen to fly in, hover around him and, in a matter of seconds, fly off again. This was taken by those who witnessed it as a sure sign that the devil, Beelzebub, the Lord of the Flies, had arrived to claim de Rais' soul for his own. True or false? Who knows, but if nothing else, it adds to the wealth of magickal myths and legends surrounding this man and the era in which he lived.

Chapter 10
The Sorcerer Priests

It is natural that in the early pre-Christian days, at least, priests and sorcerers were regarded as one and the same thing. They assumed a role that we would interpret as that of a shaman, resulting in the assimilation of sorcerers into the priesthood. It was a logical progression, which is typified by the traditions of the witch-doctors/shamans seen in Native American, South American, African and Asian cultures. These are traditions that still exist in a diluted form today and may well even outlast the recent addition of the three monotheistic faiths. The other factor here is that the spiritual and, to some extent, temporal needs of individual groups were attended to by this caste of sorcerer priests who were aware that they wielded considerable authority. The fact was not lost on them and they cultivated it and through a natural, almost evolutionary, process, they were elevated by popular consent to the rank of either a ruler or king, which, in turn, led to the formation of dynasties. This frequently resulted in a measure of arrogance, which, over time, allowed individual rulers to assume that the position was theirs by right and disconnecting from the population.

They were obviously aware that they had to remain in control and this led to the creation of a politico/magickal priesthood, subordinate to the king, that could reinforce the position and influence of the ruling dynasty using various forms of magick, including augury and healing. This continued to be the case for millennia, except in some instances there were variants where the king was ritually murdered to ensure the renewal and growth of the harvest. The tradition of priest/kings continued in one form or another and, eventually, rather than the king being killed to ensure a good harvest, in some cases, the king was killed when he became weak. Depending on the culture, this could be interpreted in a number of ways. In some cases, injuries and scars suffered in battle were enough (the king had to be perfect) and even the ageing process was sufficient. Gradually, the traditions withered and faded and other belief systems took hold and this included the faiths that worshipped a single, all-powerful god and, as far as we are concerned, this included the development of Christianity from Judaism and, through the intervention of Constantine, who made it the state religion of Rome, thus emerged the Roman Catholic Church.

Although the Church absorbed many belief systems into its own canon of dogma, as we have seen, it would not tolerate any form of deviation from its doctrine and did its very best to eliminate heresy by any means possible.

Nevertheless, there were still those among its legions of priests who found the attractions and accessibility offered by the 'dark side' irresistible. Why this state of affairs came about is unclear, but it may have been created by a mixture of the 'forbidden fruit' syndrome combined with the Church doctrine of celibacy enforced on those who chose to represent it. Whether or not celibacy is acceptable or even desirable is a very debatable point, but there are two (and possibly three) ways of looking at it. The early church father, Tertullian, first mooted the idea circa 200AD, although it may have existed before this, but at the Council of Elvira, circa 225AD, it was carefully considered and the decision was made that married priests (and there were many) should not have sexual intercourse with their wives.

Actually, the subjects dealt with by the early Councils of the Church are interesting, for it was here that the Church first moved to separate itself from the magickal beliefs that lay at its inception and, to some extent, influenced how its officers thought. For example, at the Council of Laodicea, in 364AD, decisions were taken, specifically forbidding priests from becoming or having truck with magicians, enchanters, astrologers and, strangely enough, mathematicians, which shows just how much the Church distrusted and feared the science of mathematics and the inconvenient truths it revealed about the world around it. Slightly later, in 525AD, at the Council of Oxia, laws were enacted, forbidding the consultation of sorcerers, wizards and diviners and the use of various tools that were used in divination. At the Council of Tours, in 613AD, since religion and the old beliefs still conflicted, it was decided that priests should actively promote the official policy that magick was no substitute for prayer and this decision was expanded on at most of the later Church Councils and the process still continues today. Later still, in 692AD, at the Council of Constantinople, because people still persisted in using diviners, rules were enacted, temporarily excommunicating diviners, fortune tellers and those who consulted them for a period of six years.

The matter of priestly celibacy was further considered at the 1st Council of Nicea, circa 325AD, where it was decided that this was the best policy, since it encouraged physical and spiritual 'purity' (whatever that means) and stopped domestic matters influencing the spiritual contemplations and judgements of priests. From then on, it became part of Church dogma and so it has continued, for better or worse, ever since, although affairs between priests and females in their flock surface regularly in the news. The second possible explanation is much more logical and pragmatic and it has been suggested that the decision was reached purely to prevent wives or children laying any claim to Church assets or finances. The third, apparently pious, but potentially explosive, reason is that since, according to Church dogma, Christ was not married, then his representatives should attempt to emulate this by not marrying either. Finally, it has been suggested that a build-up of sexual tension through celibacy is a powerful adjunct to magick. The Council of Nicea and its world-changing fallout will crop up again a little later.

This interpretation is, of course, is an absolute minefield, because there is already a body of persuasive evidence, albeit speculative, suggesting that Christ was, indeed, married to Mary Magdalene and may well have had children. The Church, quite naturally, denounces and denies this in the clearest possible terms, but their denials may stem from the implication that, if Christ was married and did have a family, then it flies in the face of the teaching that Christ was an avatar, i.e. a god manifesting as a human being. It also suggests that for Christ to have married and have children, rather than make him more believable, it would render him less than unique and also hints that he was 'impure', non-spiritual and capable of human failings. After all, what possible need could a god have for a human female partner? All of these explanations have their attractions, but the latter seems to have a certain logic about it and it has certainly caused much feverish speculation recently.

The Church itself, perhaps because of the ideas and concepts taught to its priests, while training, produced numerous individuals with ideas contrary to its dogma. Sometimes this occurred while they were still in the process of training, in which case they were either dismissed or left of their own accord, but, occasionally, these ideas did not surface until much later. This led to many priests continuing to preach, but without any real conviction and, in more extreme cases, these priests began to preach their own version of the gospel, which, of course, led to their expulsion (if not imprisonment and death) for heresy. In the instances where the punishment of dismissal was thought sufficient, the renegade priests were 'defrocked' and forbidden to preach. Among those who were defrocked, a few decided to turn their knowledge to an alternative path and took an deep interest in the occult and magick. This would have been quite natural to them, especially in terms of ritual magick, since they were already accustomed to the elaborate rituals associated with the worship of God. As we will see, the fact that a priest has been forbidden to carry out his pastoral duties or say Mass does not make him any less a priest.

I should make it crystal clear that although these practices have gone on for generations, we do not have the space or time to account for them all here, so, to illustrate the point, we should perhaps consider what was one of the most blatant and notorious examples (among many) of the deliberate perversion of religion to suit the desires of those with an insatiable lust for power and influence. This began in 17th Century France during the reign of King Louis XIV and continued, in one form or another, for almost 150 years. It also serves to clearly demonstrate how the rituals observed during religious services, in particular those of the Catholic Church, were the inspiration for those used in magickal ceremonies, especially those dedicated to requesting the aid of Satan and his demons. Before continuing with the details, we should ask what is required to conduct such a ceremony? Since the purpose of such a rite is designed to enlist the aid of 'dark forces', then there should be something designed for use in a religious service dedicated to good that can be defiled and debased in the hope that this will attract negativity.

In the context of an era when religion was actually a living, breathing part of day-to-day life, this came in various forms. In some instances, it involved the use of garments intended for use during the Mass, in which case they would be modified to include various signs and symbols specifically dedicated to Satan. They were considered especially effective if they had actually been used to say a Mass. In addition to this was the use of a consecrated host used, or intended for use, during the sacrament of Holy Communion. These were considered vital because, according to the traditions of the Catholic Church, prior to Holy Communion and during transubstantiation, they became the literal body and blood of Christ.

Lest there is any confusion here and at the risk of being repetitious, in reality and as far as the Church is concerned, during the sacrifice of the Mass, the metaphorical crucifixion of Christ is carried out every time the sacrament of Holy Communion is observed. This is in order that the faithful can identify with the enormity and sheer cruelty of what was done to their spiritual master - it is the sacrifice of the lamb, of the pure, of the innocent. Make no mistake about it, as far as Catholic doctrine is concerned, Christ is actually and literally present on the altar in the form of bread and wine and He is in the tabernacle (i.e. the house of God), so in fact, God is also present on the altar. Every time Catholics attend Mass and look at the altar, they are looking at the earthly house and sanctuary of God. These are extremely dramatic and evocative statements, but are exact parallels with what happens during some magickal rituals where sacrifice is involved and although the intent may be different, it is, nevertheless, entirely magickal.

Priests and their assistants dispensing Holy Communion were warned to watch out for those receiving the sacrament either hiding the communion wafer in their hands or not swallowing it for later removal. Surprisingly enough, the injunction is still in force today, although the likelihood of anyone stealing a wafer is considerably less than it once was. Alternatively, in medieval times, if an ordained priest could be persuaded to consecrate a number of hosts for illicit use, then so much the better, but, if found out, any priest who did so would automatically forfeit any claim to the priesthood and face expulsion from the Church and possible execution. It has been suggested that a defrocked priest could fulfil the same function, but, for purists, this would be ineffective, since the words, if spoken by someone who was profane, such as a layman or an excommunicated priest, would be ineffective and the 'holy magick' would not occur. This is not the case in magickal rituals where a defrocked priest is almost a prerequisite for an invocation to be effective. As already mentioned, just because a priest is defrocked, it does not mean he suddenly forget his training.

This leads us rather neatly to one of the powerful similarities between the standard method of consecrating communion wafers and the use of magickal spells and concerns the use of specific words. It is an exact parallel with the use of magickal 'words of power' like the Tetragrammaton. Prior to Holy Communion, the officiating priest must be fully ordained and he must speak the words in Latin for them to be effective, because, at that point, the priest acts as a channel or conduit for Christ who, spiritually at least, is present on the altar, so, in effect, the priest effectively becomes Christ by reciting the words (spell/formula?). The words are, "Hoc est enim corpus meum" ("For this is my body") and "Hic est enim calix sanguinis mei" ("For this is the chalice of my blood") and there is no deviation from this. These were the very words used by Christ at the Last Supper when he prepared communion for his disciples.

This was highlighted following the Second Ecumenical Council of the Vatican (better known as 'Vatican II'), which lasted from 1962 until 1965, when it became permissible to say the Mass in whatever language was appropriate to the country in which it was celebrated. This presents at least one complication, the language that Christ would have used to say these words at the Last Supper was Aramaic, which was his ethnic language, and not Latin. The official answer to this is that the Latin translation has, over time, become charged with spiritual authority and, therefore, carries the same weight and gravitas. While initially seeming a dubious explanation, it does have magickal precedence in that artefacts also, apparently, become charged with spiritual power merely through custom and practice, in other words, faith, which may account for the results claimed for sacred relics etc. Strangely enough, the ultra-conservative Curia of the Vatican, although initial resistant to the profound changes of Vatican II, largely acquiesced and allowed their eventual adoption into Church dogma. This led to some fevered speculation, because it is reasonable to assume that if they let it happen, then it must have suited their ends to do so, although the reason why is not quite so clear.

Prior to this and irrespective of location, all Masses were read in Latin in what was termed the 'Tridentine Mass' and, in spite of official opposition from the Vatican, this version of the Mass still exists in some quarters, although to perform it can lead to excommunication. The use of the Tridentine Mass is arguably a good policy, since it ensures uniformity and cohesion, but the Vatican decided it was more appropriate for those attending the Mass to understand what was happening, which is a view that also has its attractions. The only part of the service that was not changed were the words spoken during the consecration of the host, because they were regarded as essential for the transformation to occur.

That Masses were used for magickal practices is indisputable, although there will doubtless be those who would interpret this differently in that these ceremonies were used for 'good' purposes rather than 'evil' ones. For these 'Black Masses', the sanctified holy oil or 'chrism', used during legitimate services, along with consecrated wine, is also used if available. If they can be obtained, they are corrupted with other substances, but if not, then they can be substituted using urine, blood or anything else thought suitable. A toad can replace the consecrated wafer or even a slice of blackened turnip cut in the shape of a pentagram and, occasionally, the wafer is made from dried excrement.

Although at first sight an abomination, the last substitution has been justified on the grounds that excrement has the potential to support and promote growth in terms of plant life etc. This justification is also used where the sex act takes place during the ceremony, because of the obvious associations with fertility and life. Then, of course, there is the altar. During a Satanic ritual or Black Mass (and the two are not always necessarily the same), the altar can be the body of a woman, usually naked, and the service is conducted on her body. This usually involves the celebrant having sex with the woman at some point. Perhaps we should not be too hasty to make judgements regarding this type of ceremony, because all Masses, or indeed any kind of religious service, Christian or otherwise, are said with the intention of altering reality to suit a defined purpose and just because one deity is chosen over another or a particular ritual is employed, does not alter the facts one bit. Masses are said for the sick and dying, to bring about an end to conflict, to save those in distress and even, in extreme cases, to wish ill on someone. No matter how one attempts to justify it, this is still magick.

In addition to what we have seen here, there are at least two more instances where 'Bible magick' has been used for the benefit of individuals by attempting to force a change in the natural order of things through harnessing the name of God for their own ends using the 'Mass of the Holy Spirit'. This belief, which traces its origins back to the first Jesuit school in Messina, circa 1548, emerges from the depths of ancient traditions and folk magick, especially in medieval France, which held that Catholic priests had secret knowledge of specific commands, rites and invocations that could control the elements of wind, fire and water. Irrespective of the justification, such was the taboo against saying this Mass that any priest attempting to do so and commanding such powerful elemental forces had to seek absolution from his perceived sins upon completion of the ritual. Perhaps this served to put the genie (djinn) 'back in the bottle' so to speak. It has to be said, though, that even then, the more secularly-minded priests refused to perform the Mass of the Holy Spirit, which, of course, presumes that it actually existed in the first place. However, evidently Capuchin monks, supposedly being more spiritually aware, were considered more amenable to requests from those who seemed to require such a magickal ritual and, in theory at least, were, therefore, more inclined to perform it. This relationship between the people and their priests hints at the unthinking and trusting rapport between the sorcerer priests of old and the local community.

There is, however, another alleged ritual that can be used. This is the considerably more sinister and baleful 'Mass of Saint Secaire', which, if true, clearly shows the 'dark side' of religion and how it really can be hijacked for evil. It has to be said that this is a little-known ritual, even among the priesthood, and of those who are aware of it, only very few, if any, would even consider conducting it. The Mass, which originates in Gascony, France, appears to be another parody of the Catholic Mass and would be conducted by a defrocked priest using a prostitute (or his lover) as an assistant. The Mass is conducted in a ruined or deconsecrated church and said backwards, starting at exactly 11pm and ending at midnight. Communion is said using a triangular, black host and the sacramental wine is taken from a well into which has been thrown the dead body of an un-baptised infant and when the sign of the cross is made, it is on the ground using the left foot. On completion, the subject of the malediction starts wasting away with no obvious physical sign of illness and the outcome is always fatal.

Jesus the Magician

One of the possibilities surrounding sorcerer priests within Christian traditions might even stem from almost unthinkable claims made about Jesus Christ, i.e. that he was a sorcerer and was crucified for that reason and not for claiming he was the Son of God or that he was a political dissenter and general troublemaker. Is there any evidence for this? First, as we have seen, the use of any technique that causes a spontaneous change to occur with no good or obvious reason, irrespective of whether it is good or bad, is, by definition, magick. This applies specifically to the miracles performed by Jesus, whether it was changing water into wine at the wedding feast at Canaan or feeding the five thousand, these are still clear displays of supernatural ability and, therefore, magick. This is also true of other magickal biblical heroes like King Solomon and his original Temple and even Moses parting the Red Sea, but those attributed to Jesus are particularly apt, not least since Jesus is supposedly one facet of Almighty God and, therefore, theoretically at least, potentially the most influential and effective of all magicians before or since.

Unfortunately, the proof that these events actually occurred is, in itself, problematic, due to frequent differences and contradictions in the Talmud with reference to Jesus. In some cases, he is referred to as Yeshua Bin Pandrea (sometimes expressed as Pantera) and in others as Yeshua Ben (or Bin) Stada and these figures were not necessarily around at the same time. These accounts are not in accordance with accepted scripture either and are only found in pseudepigraphal gospels. These are stories, which, in the Catholic tradition, are called 'apocryphal', found in accounts such as 'The Gospel of

Nicodemus', that were not adopted by the official Greek version of scripture. In this gospel, while Jesus stands trial before Pilate, the Jews accuse Him of healing on the Sabbath by means of sorcery. According to his accusers, "He is a sorcerer and, by Beelzebub, the prince of the devils, He casteth out devils, and they are all subject unto Him."

These assertions made by His accusers may not have been true, but designed instead to further blacken His name and provide yet another reason to have Him killed. The additional judicial poison was used because, being a political agitator, although serious, was not necessarily a capital offence, nor, as far as the Romans were concerned, was claiming to be King of the Jews, but being a sorcerer or 'malificus' was. In addition, the punishment of death by crucifixion was fully recognised by the Romans for the truly agonising and protracted death that it was and it was reserved for only the most hardened criminals, enemies of Rome or... magicians; therefore, if found guilty of sorcery, the agenda of the Jewish Council, the Sanhedrin, who absolutely rejected the very idea of Jesus as King, would be served. The horrific agony of crucifixion even found its way into the lexicon of the English language in words like 'excruciating', derived from 'ex crucis' or 'of the cross'.

Although these differences are there, irrespective of which Yeshua/Jesus is mentioned, both are claimed to be sorcerers and/or miracle workers, depending on the kind of political 'spin' being put upon them. For example, Bin Stada is quoted as bringing magickal techniques, specifically witchcraft, from Egypt by scratching the sigils, words and formulae into his skin. This is, presumably, black magick. Alternatively, he is also claimed to have worked his magick using the authority of the secret name of God, the Tetragrammaton (white magick?), which he copied from the foundation stone of Solomon's Temple onto parchment and smuggled back with him. If all this is true, then it indicates that magick is part and parcel of the foundations of Christianity and this is something that would be absolute anathema to the Church.

In addition to this, in Sanhedrin 43A of the Talmud, there is mention of a 'Yeshu':

There is a tradition (in a Barraitha): They hanged Yeshu on the Sabbath of the Passover. But for forty days before that, a herald went in front of him (crying), "Yeshu is to be stoned because he practiced sorcery and seduced Israel and led them away from God. Anyone who can provide evidence on his behalf should come forward to defend him." When, however, nothing favourable about him was found, he was hanged on the Sabbath of the Passover.

Is this the same person? It seems likely, but perhaps the last word on magician priests originates from the outrageous and unlikely claims made by 'televangelists', who present self-serving television shows such as 'Airs TV',

'EWTV' and others like them, broadcast mainly on the satellite television 'God channels'.

On these programmes, the presenters blatantly advertise such products as the Don Stewart Prosperity Faith Handkerchief, which is a green square of cloth bearing the monogram 'DS'. This ostensibly free piece of cloth, once 'charged with power' in a manner similar to the aforementioned Nazi 'Blood Banner', is guaranteed to produce money from nowhere and allow those with faith to pay off all their debts. The presenter, the titular Don Stewart, who also styles himself as an apostle, takes one handkerchief and holds it in his hand, apparently charging it with faith, then touches other handkerchiefs with it. The methodology is identical to that of the Blood Banner. Just for good measure, he also requires that you let him have your name, so that he can bless that as well. This seems to be a nod to the belief that possessing someone's name gives a degree of control over them.

His TV programme also shows apparently miraculous cures of people in the audience, including one soul who, after being touched by Rev Stewart, throws aside his crutches, leaps to his feet and runs around, apparently effortlessly. The Rev Stewart touches (heals?) another audience member, who promptly pushes away his Zimmer frame and literally leaps into the air and touches his toes, once again with no apparent difficulty. Those who have been 'healed' loudly declare that, only moments previously, they were practically immobile... powerful (if unlikely) magick indeed. Yet another audience member is 'slain in the spirit', throws their arms around wildly and then falls to the floor, to be assisted by helpers hovering in the vicinity.

Another unlikely product that receives considerable attention is featured on a show aired by 'Faith TV', this time offering free samples of an apparently miraculous product called Miracle Olive Oil Soap, which, once again, practically guarantees wealth and healing when one washes with it. This is offered in conjunction with a package of religious themed goods called the Prosperity Prayer Package, especially reduced from almost $100 to $22.95. This collection of CDs and a book also offers substantial financial and heath gains when you accept God into your life, although the prospect of redemption seems as if it has been grafted on almost as an afterthought and secondary to the money. Incidentally, the comparison with the infamous Blood Banner is not intended as a reflection on either the Prosperity Faith Handkerchief or the Rev Stewart, but it does serve to demonstrate the ways in which magick is exploited in everyday life and how its eventual application depends on the user.

In almost all of these shows, near weeping individuals (mostly female) are introduced, each telling of how riches and good fortune came their way shortly after receiving one of these scraps of green cloth - a magickal item indeed. Another dubious product also touted as a sure-fire path to riches and, of course, a closer union with Almighty God, is the Miracle Spring Water &

Anointed Faith Tool, which promises that, if used appropriately, God will bless you with money and success. Magick it seems is only a phone call away and even the call is free. A win win situation? Perhaps, but it is doubtful in the extreme. Looked at from another perspective, all of this sounds rather like the remarkable claims made for the so-called magickal symbols and charms sold through some New Age magazines and is, probably, just as effective. If one takes the time to step back and evaluate this kind of naked exploitation, it quickly becomes obvious that these claims are founded squarely on greed and the desire (by the gullible) to acquire money by any means possible.

Perhaps the most blatant example of this kind of rampant exploitation is the hard sell on the INITV channel, which promotes the impression that God will cancel your debts and provide a 'financial anointing' if only you will take up the phone, call the free-phone number and give them $1,000 (or £600) as a 'favour seed' (as they call it) that will soon grow into untold (but heavily-implied financial) blessings for the giver. The salesman (I refuse to dignify him with the titles of pastor, reverend or minister) then proceeds to demonstrate the vaguest kind of clairvoyance by 'sensing' that there is someone out there with real estate issues/financial problems and they will be removed by God or that God will see to it that your loan comes through. Miracles, magick or sheer hypocritical and exploitative nonsense?

One of the best-known of those who perform these dubious 'ministries' is the Reverend Benny Hinn, who, through 'Benny Hinn Ministries', regularly performs 'healing in the spirit' and banishing demons on those present at his well-attended (and frequently televised) services. It is evidently a profitable business to be in. Healing in the spirit is a close relation to the other phenomenon of 'slaying in the spirit', where an individual is touched or sometimes breathed on by the healer and falls to the ground, having been rendered unconscious. In this case, the end result does not automatically produce dramatic scenes of frothing and shrieking, as can happen during other charismatic/evangelical Pentecostal ministries, who also claim to banish demons through the inrush of the Holy Spirit. However, the flamboyant services conducted by Rev Hinn do not impress others of a similar persuasion, who furiously denounce him for invoking demons to produce these 'healings' and castigate his entire ministry and all its works as demonic in nature.

Worse still, they say Rev Hinn is a false prophet and tainted by Catholicism, which, by their lights, is evidently even worse that being demonic. They draw this conclusion because Hinn, although originally in the Greek Orthodox Church prior to converting to Pentecostal theology, admits attending Roman Catholic educational facilities in Israel, which contributed to a rather different world view than that of his detractors, who view the Catholic faith as inherently Satanic and the Pope, any Pope, as the embodiment of the Antichrist. Neither group will admit (or are incapable of realising) that what they do and the results they obtain, irrespective of where it draws its power, is genuinely magickal in nature. It also portrays monotheistic religion in an extremely unhelpful, divided, wealth obsessed, intransigent and, ultimately, tragic fashion.

This kind of fake religion tied to magick and miracles reflects poorly on the shameful techniques used by the 'God salesmen' and, perhaps more worryingly, it also demonstrates just how gullible some sections of the population actually are. I have to say that, not being averse to receiving some easy money, as an experiment, I did call the free-phone number on the TV screen and asked if this largesse was guaranteed, since it was backed by God, and, if by some chance, I did not get the promised miracle, could I please have my money back? There was a short silence and the eventual answer was no, I could not get my money back. I continued by saying that since God was involved, then surely it had to be a guaranteed success, but, to my disappointment, they put the phone down. Some enquiries showed that this type of miracle and magick selling works quite well in the USA, but less so in the more cynical UK. Incidentally, it is unclear what actually happens to the money that is sent, but the 'salesman' looked very well-fed and well-dressed indeed.

Chapter 11
Fr. Urbain Grandier

Although we will come across a number of former priests who officiated at magickal ceremonies a little later, at this point we should consider an instance where a priest, who was neither unfrocked nor excommunicated, was accused of witchcraft and sorcery, the archetypal sorcerer priest. This was the unfortunate Fr. Urbain Grandier. Typical of such cases, it uses lurid claims of raising demons and casting spells, plus the almost inevitable additions of sex and debauchery to make its point and, bearing in mind the superstitious nature of the medieval Church plus its attitude to sex in general, this should be no surprise. The case is normally presented as a mixture of hysteria combined with a personal vendetta, which resulted in a travesty of justice and has been written about by Aldous Huxley in his 1952 book, *The Devils of Loudon*, and filmed in 1971 as *The Devils* by Ken Russell, but it is worth re-examining to see if there is any possible justification for the claims made about Fr Grandier. The case is believed to be one of the most prolific examples of demonic possession ever recorded. As we will see, the whole thing may indeed have been a charade, an elaborate and protracted act of revenge or, on the other hand, there may well have been a genuinely magickal element to it.

Urbain Grandier, who was born in 1590, served as parish priest in the French town of Loudon, in the diocese of Poitiers, where, in addition to being something of a rebellious free sprit, he chose to largely ignore his vow of celibacy and openly conducted affairs with at least two local women. Because both of the women were linked to the Royal Court through their fathers, ultimately these exploits indirectly led to his downfall. Grandier was evidently an extremely handsome man, independently wealthy, well educated and he also had good political connections, an asset that served him well. In openly flaunting the rules of celibacy, he caused considerable outrage and open hostility (or perhaps jealousy) among the Catholic hierarchy of the area and, in 1630, he was arrested on charges of immorality. It was at this point that his political connections saved him and he was discharged and restored to his position as parish priest once more. Grandier's main adversary, the Bishop of Poitiers, had presided over the proceedings while he stood trial and made no secret of the fact that he wanted him out of his diocese. What happened next is something of a mystery and there are two versions of what happened, although, either way, Grandier was put to death at the stake.

In the first version of events, it is speculated that, given the manner in

which those suspected of sorcery or witchcraft were treated, the Bishop of
Poitiers approached the confessor to the local convent of Ursuline nuns, a
Father Mignon, and asked him to persuade the Mother Superior, Jeanne des
Anges (or Sister Jeanne of the Angels) to help him. Before continuing, it is
worth pausing to note that the practice of adopting false names after joining
Holy Orders matches the practice of doing the same thing when joining a
magickal order like the Order of The Golden Dawn, where members adopted
the titles Brother or Sister along with any name they thought appropriate. At
any rate, Father Mignon approached the Mother Superior who agreed to say
that Fr Grandier had bewitched her, causing her to take fits and fall to the
ground, curse, swear and 'speak in tongues'. It is strange that, in this case,
speaking in tongues (a phenomenon now referred to as 'glossolalia') was
used to indicate possession by some malign entity, because, in modern times
at least, Pentecostalists claim this is a sure sign that those so affected have
been chosen as a channel for the Holy Spirit. Obviously, at the time of the
Loudon Possessions, this was not the case and such displays were assumed to
be demonic.

The other version suggests that Sister Jeanne had already heard about the
sexual exploits of Grandier and, having had some contact with him during
pastoral visits to the convent, found him extremely attractive and developed
an obsession about him. In a direct parallel with the demonic incubus, this
caused her to dream about Grandier in the guise of a 'bright angel', who
came to her in the night and persuaded her to have sex with him. This caused
her to cry out in her sleep, which the other nuns could hear. The Mother
Superior was horrified at these overtly sexual dreams and the illicit pleasure
she obtained from them and performed drastic penances, including
flagellation, to assuage herself from the taint of perceived sin. She then
discovered that other nuns in the convent were having similar dreams, so she
sent for their confessor, Father Mignon, to exorcise the convent of demons.
It is here that yet another level of possibilities appears.

Were these dreams signs of genuine possession or did Fr Mignon, who was
well aware that his Bishop still wanted Grandier out of the way, decide to
manipulate the events to suit his own ends? Another curious omission is that
Fr Mignon and the Mother Superior failed to make a connection with the
lusty predations of an incubus, which, given their determination to find some
evidence of Grandier's guilt, is strange. At the time, it was considered
perfectly possible (although totally undesirable) that men and women were
visited in their sleep by male and female demons, the incubus and the
succubus, who would have illicit sex with them.

The result of these illicit, nocturnal liaisons supposedly resulted in the birth
of a human/demon hybrid child, which was taken by the forces of evil for
their own nefarious purposes. This was the explanation devised by a religious
system that regarded sex as basically unclean to explain natural events like

nocturnal emissions and other unconscious sexual manifestations. It is a type of reasoning that still finds resonances today, with the claims made for the alleged insemination of human women by alien males or with men being coerced into having sex with alien females. The resultant offspring are also removed from the host mother for purposes unknown. Similar tales emerge of encounters with 'fairies' and other supernatural creatures, where the offspring of the humans is taken and replaced with a halfling baby, often referred to as a 'changeling'.

Whatever the reason, led by Fr Mignon, the exorcisms went ahead and Mother Superior Jeanne des Anges promptly began fitting, frothing and making overtly sexual overtures to the exorcists. The Mother Superior insisted that she and the other nuns, sixteen in all, were possessed by two demons, Asmodeus and Zabulon, both sent by Grandier to cause them grief. Sensing that trouble was brewing, Fr Grandier wrote to the Archbishop of Bordeaux, who, in turn, sent his own doctor to examine the nuns. The doctor travelled to the convent and conducted his examinations, but could find no sign of 'genuine possession' (presumably this included hearing them speak in an unknown tongue or act in a bizarre fashion, but, unfortunately, the method is not recorded) and when the Archbishop heard this, he ordered that the exorcisms be stopped and had the nuns locked in their cells and kept there. This lifted the immediate threat of action and arrest from Grandier, but this respite was only temporary, because the storm clouds were still gathering and getting closer all the time.

Although due to his connections Grandier's enemies had been unable to make their accusations stick. One of them, Jean de Laubardemont, a relative of the Mother Superior, was also a favourite of the powerful and scheming Cardinal Richelieu, so, along with a Capuchin monk, Fr. Tranquille, he arranged to visit Richelieu with the news that the exorcisms had been unsuccessful. While giving this information, the two priests reminded the cardinal that Grandier had penned a libellous satire about the cardinal in 1618, something that had initially angered him, but there were other facts that may well have been the final blows. In addition to Laubardemont, Richelieu also had a relative, Sister Claire, in the Loudon convent, but this was not the final reason, which was entirely political and, therefore, of far greater importance to Richelieu. While serving in Loudun, on the orders of the Cardinal, de Laubardemont was instructed to ensure the town's fortifications were destroyed, which was part of Richelieu's master plan to completely eliminate any chance that the Huguenots (Protestants) might use them to stage an uprising.

The local residents, both Catholic and Huguenot, were against the proposal, because it would leave them at the mercy of any invading forces and, at that politically unstable time, this was always a real danger. Grandier took a defiant stance about this and reminded Laubardemont that the king had guaranteed that the walls and fortifications would not be removed and, to much popular acclaim, stopped the work from going ahead. All of these factors, taken together, convinced Richelieu to set up a Royal Commission to arrest and investigate Grandier as a witch, with his recently humiliated enemy, Laubardemont, appointed as head of the commission. The exorcisms were also reinstated and, this time, publicly. The spectacle afforded by the exorcisms was something that greatly appealed to the citizens of Loudon as free entertainment and carried powerful echoes of the public executions that drew large crowds both in Europe and Britain.

The exorcisms resumed almost immediately and were conducted by Father Tranquille, a Franciscan monk called Father Lactance and a Jesuit priest, Father Jean-Joseph Surin, with up to seven thousand spectators in attendance. The exorcists were obviously delighted to have such a large and enthusiastic audience and made great play of conducting the rituals in a dramatic fashion, while encouraging the nuns to ever more lurid confessions, 'for the benefit of their souls and the banishment of Satan', as the official records have it.. The public exorcisms served the Church admirably, since it could be seen to actively combat the Devil and simultaneously reinforce its spiritual and temporal power. For Fr Surin, this was his second attempt at exorcising the nuns, his first attempt, in 1632, had ended badly for him and it is this event that causes serious concern that the possessions were not invented for political reasons or personal grudge. During the 1632 exorcism, Fr Surin decided the best way to bring about the desired result was to invite the entities into his own body, thereby freeing the nuns. When he did this, he quickly displayed signs of insanity and began to harm himself and this went as far as attempting suicide. He later recovered his senses, but claimed to have no recollection of what had transpired when the invading spirit took over.

As the exorcisms continued a remarkable number of demons were named, including Asmodeus, Zabulon, Isacaaron (appropriately enough the devil of lust and debauchery), Astaroth, Gresil (associated with lack of cleanliness and impurity), Amand, Leviatom, Behemot, Beherie, Easas, Celsus, Acaos, Cedon, Alex, Naphthalim, Cham, Ureil and Achas. Another recorded result of the ongoing exorcisms were the actions of the nuns who reportedly, "Struck their chests and backs with their heads, as if they had their necks broken, and with inconceivable rapidity. They twisted their arms at the joints of the shoulder, the elbow or the wrist, two or three times around. Lying on their stomachs, they joined the palms of their hands to the soles of their feet; their faces became so frightful one could not bear to look at them; their eyes remained open without winking. Their tongues issued suddenly from their mouths, horribly swollen, black, hard and covered with pimples and, yet, while in this state, they spoke distinctly. They threw themselves back till their heads touched their feet and walked in this position with wonderful rapidity, and for a long time. They uttered cries so horrible and so loud that nothing like it was ever heard before. They made use of expressions so indecent as to shame the most debauched of men, while their acts, both in exposing themselves and inviting lewd behaviour from those present, would have astonished the inmates of the lowest brothels in the country."

If these accounts, written in 1634, by a chronicler named des Niau, are a factual account of what he saw, then it is less likely that the actions of the nuns were faked, because they seem to mirror certain events that occurred relatively recently, during appearances of the Blessed Virgin Mary (BVM) at the towns of Medjugorje in Bosnia-Herzegovina and, to a lesser degree, at Fatima in Portugal. It is also reported that in Garabandal, following the appearance of the BVM, the children who had seen her sporadically ran backwards at great speed with their heads tilted right back, staring at the sky. Despite these bizarre sprints, they reportedly neither fell nor faltered and apparently knew exactly where they were going. Bear in mind that these were narrow and, in some cases, unpaved and uneven streets and lanes and the displays alarmed the local people, especially the children's parents, who were obviously concerned for their safety. It is obviously on a much smaller scale, but the physical feats seem to mirror those displayed by the nuns.

Eventually, Grandier was judged to have acted along with demonic forces and, in 1663, he was imprisoned in Angiers to await trial and learn his fate. To his further dismay, he realised that this was not a secular court, but one held under the terms of the Royal Commission, convened by Cardinal Richelieu. Since he was now beyond the help and influence of his powerful friends, as with all witches and sorcerers, he was 'tested' and put to the 'extraordinary question'. This specific difference meant that the tortures used under the precise regulations dictated by the Malleus Maleficarum were likely to be fatal, but not immediately and were reserved for those destined for execution anyway. In normal circumstances, i.e. being interrogated using the 'ordinary' question, anyone accused of sorcery or witchcraft could confess right away to avoid unnecessary suffering, but even with the additional savagery, Grandier steadfastly refused to name any accomplices or admit guilt.

This led the inappropriately named Father Tranquille to add to his torment by piously breaking both of Grandiers legs (a 'kindness' normally awarded to those being crucified to hasten their end), but still he would not confess. As the trial continued, more and more witnesses were called, but, unfortunately for Grandier, witnesses called for his defence found it expedient to absent themselves from the province on the grounds that it had been publicly stated that anyone speaking in his defence would be assumed a traitor to the king and arrested with all their properties being forfeit.

Among the items of evidence produced by the prosecution was a written pact supposedly between Grandier and Satan, which read as follows:

mlE ntvL bbzlB ntS entvuj rfcL snetpp soN
tcap tpecca smebah eidh qsila toratsA qta
mecillop ciuh te .e sibon iuq rdnarG brU siredeof.
po te pulov noh nom suced munigriv merolf lum meroma
lemes terffo sboN .re arac illi teirbe oudirt bacinrof
te ealccE as baclucoc sdep bus gis gas ona ni
xilef giv na teviv tcap q ;ture suispi tagor sbon
.D delam son tni aetsop nev te moh art ni
mead ssoc tni fni ni tcaF
sanataS bubezleB rfcL
imilE nahtaiveL htoratsA
mod pcnirp mead te baid gam sop giS
tprcs htrblB

This curious and damning document (effectively an admission of guilt by the beleaguered priest) is actually written in backwards Latin and includes abbreviations. In English and unabbreviated it reads:

> We, the influential Lucifer, the young Satan, Beelzebub, Leviathan, Elimi, and Astaroth, together with others, have today accepted the covenant pact of Urbain Grandier, who is ours. And him do we promise the love of women, the flower of virgins, the respect of monarchs, honors, lusts and powers.

> He will go whoring three days long; the carousal will be dear to him. He offers us once in the year a seal of blood, under the feet he will trample the holy things of the church and he will ask us many questions; with this pact he will live twenty years happy on the Earth of men, and will later join us to sin against God. Bound in hell, in the council of demons. Lucifer Beelzebub Satan Astaroth Leviathan Elimi The seals placed the Devil, the master, and the demons, princes of the lord. Baalberith, writer.

All pretty negative stuff and full of typical images of the desecration of religious items, debauchery and licentious behaviour and, as far as the debauchery is concerned, from what is known of Fr Grandier, not too far away from what he was actually doing. It is also assumed to have been written by the tormented priest, although whether this was a result of the torture is unclear. On the other hand, it could well have been a forgery. Despite this, it was only one item in an overwhelming amount of evidence against him, but it was not until a year later, in 1634, that Grandier was finally found guilty and condemned to be burned at the stake. The statement of the Royal Commission reads:

> 'We have ordered and do order the said Urbain Grandier duly tried and convicted of the crime of magic, maleficia and of causing demoniacal possession of several Ursuline nuns of this town of Loudun, as well as of other secular women, together with other charges and crimes resulting therefrom. For atonement of which, we have condemned and do condemn the said Grandier to make amende honorable, his head bare, a rope round his neck, *(this was intended for use as a garrotte with which to strangle him prior to the fire being lit, another benevolent act of 'compassion')* holding in his hand a burning taper weighing two pounds, before the principle door of the church of St. Pierre-du-Marché and before that of St. Ursual of this town. There on his knees, to ask pardon of God, the King, and the Law. This done, he is to be taken to the public square of St. Croix and fastened to a stake on a scaffold, which shall be erected on the said place for this purpose, and there to be burned alive... and his ashes scattered to the wind. We have ordered and so do order that each and every article of his moveable property be acquired and confiscated by the King, the sum of 500 livres first being taken for buying a bronze plaque on which will be engraved the abstract of this present trial, to be set up in a prominent spot in the said church of the Ursulines, to remain there for all eternity. And, before proceeding to the execution of the present sentence, we order the said Grandier to be submitted to the first and last degrees of torture, concerning his accomplices.'

Unfortunately for the priest, the demands and conditions set out in the statement were imposed to the letter.

Grandier, still unable to walk because of the severe damage inflicted to his legs, was half-dragged, half-carried from his prison cell to the locations mentioned then to his place of execution until finally he was tied to the stake. According to the available records, Grandier had been promised that he would be strangled before the flames were lit to spare him being half-suffocated by the smoke then slowly roasted alive, but the rope had, probably deliberately, been left with no slipknot in place so this did not happen.

However, the condemned man did manage a measure of revenge and this, if true, would tend to support the assertions that he really was a sorcerer. As the flames rose around him, Grandier evidently cried out that Fr. Lactance, the only one of the judges who was present at the execution, would die in thirty days. The curse was evidently effective and Lactance did die exactly thirty days later and on his deathbed sobbed, "Grandier, I was not responsible for your death." Over the next five years, the other judges, including Father Tranquille and a Dr. Mannouri, who had actually supervised the torture, died. Father Surin, who, as already mentioned, had experienced spiritual problems relating to his exorcisms of the nuns some years earlier, started to have visions of demons and ended up unable to perform day-to-day functions. He could not even pray. He even attempted suicide in 1645 and, unable to walk, was cared for by the Jesuits until he finally died in 1665.

What we have seen here happened to one Roman Catholic priest accused of sorcery and witchcraft in medieval France and judged by the Church he served. Modern interpretations of what occurred assume it to be a put-up job designed by jealous rivals to have a man they considered as immoral, impious and/or a threat to their positions legally murdered. Exactly who the 'puppet master' was pulling the strings behind the scenes is uncertain, but is assumed to have been Cardinal Richelieu, who was the only person with sufficient influence to have set the plan in motion and carry it through. But, if so, it does seem to be a case of obsessive and vengeful 'overkill', like using a very large hammer to crush a walnut.

Another explanation theorises that the possessed nuns lived in a kind of sexual manic/hysterical pressure cooker environment, created by the cloistered life they led. A condition finally and violently triggered by the frustrated obsession the Mother Superior had for the dashing Fr Grandier. Modern psychologists who, for their own reasons, favour this explanation, have quoted many similar instances where this kind of sexual and emotional hysteria has flared up in enclosed same sex institutions like prisons and even schools. It should be noted that, as mentioned right at the very start of this book, psychologists and psychiatrists will always try to ascribe unusual phenomena involving perception or altered states of awareness to any cause other than anything magickal or paranormal. It is in their interests to do so and also those of the drug companies who, in many cases, fund them. Another explanation has been proffered citing the inadvertent consumption of 'ergot' by the nuns. Ergot is a hallucinogenic parasitic fungus similar to LSD (in fact, LSD was derived from ergot in 1938 by Sandoz Labs) that can form on damp rye grain prior to being milled into flour for bread. Even after baking, the hallucinogenic effects remain and it has also been suggested that this may have played a part in the notorious Salem Witch Trials and other spontaneous outbreaks of apparently magickal events. The Salem Witch Trials and their tragic outcome were notable for having been constituted and prosecuted by Puritans and not Catholics.

These convenient, plausible and predictably rational explanations completely ignore the simple fact that Urbain Grandier may, indeed, have been a magician who, for his own reasons, decided to entrance the nuns in an Ursuline convent. Or that the nuns did become possessed by invading entities for purposes unknown. Certainly some of the evidence suggests exactly that and perhaps consuming the hallucinogen contributed to it. If shamans can converse and successfully commune with invisible creatures, including snakes, the so-called 'machine elves' and other beings, after having taken naturally hallucinogenic substances, like ayahuasca, then why not the nuns? Do not forget that the effects of taking ayahuasca are reliable, well-known and documented and produce remarkably similar effects and images in those who take it. These relatively naive women would not have known they had taken this substance nor been able to analyse the results and, therefore, if at all suggestible, it is possible that they really did have a shared, magickal experience.

Another factor is the remarkable and unsettling physical contortions the nuns displayed. These are well-known in cases of demonic possession and occur time and time again, although, once again, they have also been noted in various types of hysterical conditions. Then there is the strange pact supposedly written by Fr Grandier. Was this a prop, a mere piece of additional window dressing or is it possible that it was genuine? The use of pacts with the Devil or other powerful deities was (and to some extent still is) part of certain magickal ceremonies. There was also the successful curse cast upon Fr. Lactance by the agonised Grandier as the fire consumed him, plus the deaths of others who had plotted against him. Finally, were the two episodes where Fr. Surin suffered a nervous collapse as a result of attempting to exorcise powerful demonic forces? Was this a sign that something truly magickal was afoot?

Tales of witches and sorcerers throwing curses to their tormentors as death looms close are the stuff of legend and the effects are apparently effective. It is a matter of record that when Jacques de Molay, the last grand master of the Knights Templar, was burned at the stake, he uttered a curse, in-keeping with the aura of magick and the occult that still hangs over this most enigmatic of orders. It is said that before he died, de Molay cursed the King Philip le Bel and Pope Clement, calling for them to join him and account for themselves before the court of God within a year and, remarkably, this is exactly what happened. Less than a month later, Pope Clement was dead, supposedly from dysentery, and, by the year's end, so was King Philip. Events like these only served to further enhance the reputation of the Templars as masters of alchemy, magick and the occult arts. In spite of some revisionist history that seeks to exonerate the Templars, there can be little doubt that they did possess considerable occult knowledge and may well have used it in their own initiation ceremonies.

Finally, if the whole protracted affair concerning Grandier actually was a hoax, why was it allowed to go on for so long with all the attendant costs, which would have been considerable? It would have been much quicker, simpler and infinitely cheaper to have had Grandier simply killed by an assassin or just jailed and allowed to rot. There is no logic behind such an extravagant course of action as an act of revenge, unless those making the charges genuinely believed him, an ordained priest, to be guilty of sorcery, in which case, the whole exercise was probably justifiable and Grandier was indeed a sorcerer priest.

Chapter 12
The Magick of Exorcism

Before moving on, there is another clear indication of another connection between the Catholic Church and magickal practices, although this, once again, depends on how one interprets magick. It also depends on the use of alleged 'words of power'. At present, one of the very few mainstream religious organisations offering an approved system of exorcism (another fairly accessible form of magick) is the Catholic Church. The Protestant churches, although they officially stopped conducting services for those possessed some time ago, have changed their opinions on the matter. They are still slightly uneasy about the process of full-blown exorcisms, but are willing to conduct what they call a 'deliverance ministry', which can vary wildly depending on which schism of Protestant belief is conducting the service. These range from simple prayers and advice to all out 'fire and brimstone' ceremonies, where the afflicted person writhes around on the floor cursing, blaspheming and frequently vomiting.

The last type of service is, not surprisingly, the province of evangelical and Pentecostal ministries, mainly in the United States of America, where the individual presiding pastor seems intent on cleansing the person afflicted by having them act out a frequently alarming psychodrama in order to encourage others present to participate. Rather worryingly, some of those cleansed frequently return to have more 'demons' removed, which must surely give serous doubt regarding the psychological state of those afflicted and the motivation of the exorcist. In addition to this, those wishing deliverance from their demons often have to sign disclaimers and waivers absolving the specific church from any threat of litigation should any physical harm be sustained at the hands of the enthusiastic exorcists. Unsurprisingly, these ministries use the name of Jesus during the cleansings and this is based on the fact that, as well as being a 'word of power', Jesus was well-known for casting out demons, so for this reason too, His name is effective. Other belief systems also carry out exorcisms, even those of the Hindus and Buddhists, who worship a different pantheon of gods and masters entirely. The practice of exorcism is also present in Judaism, using selected verses from the Torah and also in Islam, using the Qur'an, where the invading entities are regarded as djinn. There are also shamanic and Wiccan forms of exorcism that are extremely effective and usually successful. Once again, this has to be regarded as the use of one form of 'approved magick' against another that is unapproved.

The difference here is that, in the Roman Catholic tradition, the use of exorcism is permissible in specific circumstances where all medical possibilities have been ruled out, but, even then, only using a specially-trained priest operating with the express permission of a bishop. As far as the Vatican is concerned, it has its own official exorcist who oversees a number of other exorcists who operate with the blessing of the Church. The best known of these is the former Vatican chief exorcist, Fr Gabriele Amorth, who was appointed in 1984 after being trained in the duties of the post by a member of the Passionist order of monks, Fr Candido Amatini, who was, at the time, the chief exorcist. Fr Amorth, who I believe was still alive at the time of writing this, founded the 'International Association of Exorcists' in 1990 and, although retiring from the priesthood in 2000, aged 75, he was awarded the honour of presidency for life of the organisation.

There is an incident regarding Fr Amorth's instructor that gives a clear insight into the matter-of-fact way in which the two men regarded demons as a clear and present danger in everyday life. It concerns an exorcism conducted by Fr Amatini at which Fr Amorth was an assistant. He writes: "We must make this abundantly clear: evil, suffering, death and hell (that is, eternal damnation in everlasting torment) are not acts of God." What Fr Amorth fails to mention here is that the 'eternal damnation in everlasting torment', if not actually acts of God must be the result of God's displeasure towards the sinner, because, if all souls must face final judgement after death and are found irredeemable and not worthy of clemency, then surely they achieve damnation and torment by God's omission rather than an overt act. To be fair, though, all of those who would fall into this category probably richly deserve this fate and, if possible, much worse.

Fr Amorth continues: "One day, Father Candido was expelling a demon. Toward the end of the exorcism, he turned to the evil spirit and sarcastically told him, 'Get out of here. The Lord has already prepared a nice, well-heated house for you!' At this, the demon answered, 'You do not know anything! It wasn't He (God) who made Hell. It was us. He had not even thought about it.' Similarly, on another occasion, while I was questioning a demon to know whether he had contributed to the creation of Hell, I received this answer: 'All of us cooperated.'" Unsurprisingly, Fr Amorth also regards angels as a real, positive and literal presence and, although they have magickal powers equal to that of demons, they, along with the demons, are ultimately subordinate to Christ and by association, since Christ is a part of the Trinity, to God. Surely, this literalist paradigm and modus operandi must qualify Fr Amorth for the title of a 'sorcerer priest'. One of Fr Amorth's favoured scriptural usages comes from the Letter of St Paul to the Philippians (2:6-11), "So that all beings in the heavens, on Earth and in the underworld should bend the knee at the name of Jesus." A command that the demon 'should kneel at the name of Jesus'. Here is a perfect example of using a word of power, in this case, Jesus, in a truly magickal sense. It is an invocation with no attempt at hiding the word away. It is neither the Tetragrammaton, nor is it the Shemhamforash, but it is the name of one of the three traditional manifestations of God and apparently powerful enough to drive out demons. It also further illustrates why deliverance ministries use the name of Jesus.

Although now an octogenarian, Fr Amorth still works for the Vatican in an advisory capacity and still conducts exorcisms. In fact, he claims to have conducted the astonishing number of fifty thousand exorcisms during his tenure at the Vatican, although this is sometimes quoted as an even more startling seventy thousand. He says that the services lasted anywhere between a few minutes to several hours and it is not certain whether or not the numbers given are based on his own efforts or are a total of all the services performed by the priests under his command. This is more likely, since the numbers of exorcisms per day would run to an average of ten, if based on fifty thousand, and correspondingly more if the number was seventy thousand. In spite of all this, Fr Amorth cannot see that what he does is, by its very nature, magickal, because all his instincts and training tell him that magick, all magick, is inherently evil. He fails to see that the words, implements and rituals he uses during exorcisms are, likewise, based on traditional magick and simply because it is dressed up in approved religious trappings does not make it any less so.

Fr Amorth's views on possession and exorcism are deep and profoundly conservative and perhaps this is the reason that he cannot accept any other interpretation than that of his church. It may also be the reason that he can continually wage a dangerous, magickal war with entities better left well alone. He considers that those afflicted may be possessed by demons or are the victims of curses that may have originated from the ill wishes of a family member, the practice of blaspheming, involvement in spiritualism or dabbling with magick and (rather bizarrely) membership of a Masonic lodge. He has also expressed the opinion that Joseph Stalin and Adolph Hitler, along with the entire Nazi hierarchy, were possessed and he also makes clear his belief that, as stated elsewhere in this book, the Nazis were intimately involved with Satanism, magick and the occult. Strangely enough, the phenomenon of 'generational curses', which can lead to entire family lines bearing a form of possession, is part and parcel of previously mentioned deliverance ministries and the exorcisms they perform. Fr Amorth's views on this are unknown.

His opinions regarding what can only be seen as an upswing in occult belief put the matter down to, "People have lost their faith and superstition, magick, Satanism or ouija boards have taken its place, which opens all the doors to the presence of demons." In this he is, of course, correct, because the instances of possession seem to have increased as the wave of popular and, in some cases, aggressive secularism continues to grow both in pace and momentum. The reason for this may even lie at the door of the monotheistic faiths themselves, because they seem to have become increasingly out of touch, apathetic and irrelevant to those they are supposed to guide and comfort.

It may be this perceived failure to allow some effective, 'hands-on' contact or union with their God that has driven the formerly faithful to seek out and embrace alternative means of achieving spiritual union with the infinite and this has resulted in a still thriving New Age movement. The priest has also said that in order to highlight the grave, spiritual danger that society is in "People need to know what we do" in terms of their chances of spiritual rescue. Strangely enough, although Fr Amorth has publicly and vociferously castigated films like the Harry Potter series of books and films for popularising belief in sorcery and magick, the Vatican decided that Harry Potter presented no danger to the spiritual well-being of the faithful.

Chapter 13
Fr Amorth and Freemasonry

Fr Amorth's choice to include Freemasonry as one of the factors allegedly contributing to possession is interesting and is worth pausing to take a look at. The Masonic movement has been around in various forms for centuries and did not just suddenly spring forth, fully-formed, when the English Grand Lodge was created on the 24th of June, 1717. What this did do, however, was formalise the various strands of Freemasonry, some of which can be traced to the 14th Century in Britain, under one banner in order to bring cohesion into the way it was structured and to ensure that the rituals were, more or less, standard. This is not the case in Scotland, where the Masonic constitution is different and there are slight variations in the degrees operated in Scottish lodges, although the key words are the same. Having said that, there are slight variations between lodges in how the words are pronounced and spelled and this is further confused when the Masonic Order in the United States operates using a constitution with the misleading title of the 'Scottish Rite', which, once again, is not the same.

The condemnation of Freemasonry by Fr Amorth is supported by years of opposition by the Catholic Church (among other religious variants) to the Masonic Order and was originally based on its assertion that the Masonic version of God is naturalistic and rational in nature, which, while carrying hints of gnosticism, is opposed to Catholic dogma. The original proscription came from Pope Clement XII in 1738 and again by Pope Leo XII in 1890, but the hammer blow for would be (or actual) Roman Catholic masons came in 1917 when the code of canon law that governs Church legislation expressly forbade membership under pain of automatic excommunication.

The situation remains unchanged, even when the liberalisation of the fateful Vatican II council appeared to indicate that it was permissible. The situation was clarified by the then Cardinal Ratzinger, who, in his position as head of the Congregation for the Doctrine of the Faith said that the Masonic Order was still at variance with Catholic teachings and those who were (or planned to be) members could no longer receive Holy Communion. So, in spite of claims to the contrary, it is effectively still banned. On the other hand, the Masonic Order has no official proscription forbidding Catholics becoming members and many are. The Protestant opposition to Freemasonry, usually, but not always, attached to fundamentalist sects, is normally based on allegations of association with mysticism, magick and even Satanism. This charge is frequently directed as such American Masonic luminaries as General Albert Pike, who did much to formalise the order in that country, as being a Satanist.

The Islamic objections (in Saudi Arabia, it is expressly forbidden to conduct Masonic ceremonies, let alone open a lodge, an edict enforced by the threat of imprisonment and/or deportation) are based on the assumption that lodges are influenced or controlled by Jewish and Zionist elements. Using this front, they are supposedly determined to destroy the Islamic Holy of Holies, the Dome on the Rock, and rebuild the Temple of Solomon. There are also claims that the 'Dajjal' is worshiped and celebrated in Masonic ceremonies. The Dajjal equates roughly to the Christian concept of the 'false messiah' and there are other similarities with the Old Testament in that the Dajjal is prophesied to appear as the 'Masih' (Messiah) prior to the End Times. This exactly parallels the concept of the Antichrist and it should, since these interpretations both come from the same scriptural source. That said, there are Masonic lodges in Saudi Arabia (albeit illicit) and they are conducted in the relative safety of the various camps and compounds that abound in that country and set aside for the accommodation of foreign technicians. Most of these lodges operate under a German constitution.

Interestingly enough, Masonic lodges were present quite legally in Iraq from approximately 1919, during the days of the British Mandate, but were forbidden following the revolution in 1958 and this continued under the tyranny of Saddam Hussein, when membership of a lodge was punishable by death. This was, once again, based on the assumed connection with Zionism and all that goes with it. However, following the overthrow of Saddam and his regime, in 2003, it was suggested that Freemasonry might be reintroduced in Iraq due to the number of Freemasons currently serving in the armed forces and working for civilian contractors. There are also legitimate lodges operating in the Muslim countries of Morocco and Turkey. The more stringent attitude found in Saudi Arabia almost certainly stems from the fact that the Saudi brand of Islam is Wahabi in nature and, therefore, much more conservative than other strands of that faith.

In spite of the official reasons given, the main issue that the Christian and, especially, Catholic objectors like Fr Amorth have with the Masonic Order comes from one word used during the Royal Arch Degree. This, they say, represents the Masonic God and the word is 'Jabulon'. There is much argument regarding what this word actually means, but the origins are steeped in mysticism and magick. The word seems to be formed from three separate deities, Ja, Bul and On, all of which are supposed to relate directly to the Hebrew deity, Yahweh, also Baal and the Egyptian god, Osiris. According to the Christian canon of belief, none of these have any connection with the Christian God and therefore are incompatible with Christianity. The Freemasons are quick to point out that, since Freemasonry is not a religion, there is no conflict. Nevertheless, there is some cause for concern here that seems to establish a link with Satan in the form of Baal. The connection between Baal and Satan is alleged to come from the pejorative term, Ba'al-zebub (or Beelzebub), as one of the many names associated with the Devil.

The word is also used in degrees operated by the overtly magickal organisation the Ordo Templi Orientis (OTO) where it appears twice with distinctly Masonic associations in degrees called, 'The Lodge of Perfection', also known as 'Prefect Magician and Companion of the Royal Arch of Enoch' and also in 'Perfect Initiate' or 'Prince of Jerusalem'. Many organisations that practice ceremonial magick, like the OTO, base their rituals around a series of initiatory degrees exactly in the manner operated by Masonic lodges. It was always seen in anything involving the magician, Aleister Crowley, who, unsurprisingly, was also a Freemason. Intriguingly, the Rastafarian word for God is Jah, although it is not known whether the same connection exists.

As regards the antipathy shown by Fr Amorth to the Masonic Order, perhaps this is because he regards it as a symptom of the present perceived liberalism of the modern Catholic Church as inferior to the organisation that existed prior to the changes introduced during Vatican II. In fact, he is quite outspoken about it and regards the revised form of exorcism, which also came from Vatican II, as "A farce, an incredible obstacle that is likely to prevent us from acting against demons." From his perspective, he is, of course, quite correct, since the new rite does not allow exorcism to be carried out on those who are judged to have been affected by 'evil spells' or maledictions and, to be fair, it is difficult to see the difference.

He also notes that (in his opinion, at least) evil spells are responsible for at least ninety percent of possessions involving demons and he sees no need to replace prayers that have been used with good results for more than a thousand years. Furthermore, he has also been quoted as saying that the Devil is at large in the Vatican. Fr Amorth was greatly pleased when Pope Benedict XIV announced the formation of what can only be regarded as exorcism 'hit squads' to tackle the perceived increase in demonic possessions. Again, it gives pause for thought to consider that, at present, Italy is seeing an upswing in alternative sources of spiritual enlightenment and fulfilment in the form of clairvoyance, fortune telling and spiritualism, especially around the northern industrial areas like Torino, so perhaps Fr Amorth has good reason to be concerned. As we have seen, these are precisely the practices denounced and proscribed at the Council of Oxia in 525AD. Does this shift in emphasis signify that the Church is losing its authority as the public continue to be seduced by the immediacy offered by face-to-face contact with the 'other side'? Might this also be viewed as a victory for Satan in gradually wooing the faithful away from God?

The magickal formula of exorcism as prescribed in Rituale Romanum (or Roman Ritual), the one much revered and used by Fr Amorth, was also a precise series of words and invocations written in Latin millennia ago and intended for use as a spell to drive out invading entities from a person or place. This carries much the same authority as the form of words used during the consecration of the host prior to the sacrament of Holy Communion. The difference here is that the language and structure have been changed in line with changes made at Vatican II. Does this mean that the prayer/invocation no longer carries the same inherent power or that its use will create that same power over a period of time, rather like a riff on the legalistic expression of something being accepted though custom and practice? Or does it indicate that the 'power' resides in the Crowleyian concept of will or Thelema and is reflected in the energy that drives Chaos Magick where the concept of 'fake it till you make it' holds true. In other words does it all depend on the sincerity, the faith if you like, of the individual priest?

The actual invocations used in the Rituale Romanum, which, incidentally, contains rather more than the formerly approved words used in exorcisms, are extremely lengthy and in Latin, so, for brevity, I have included below the revised version of the ritual and it is in English. It was also the form of words used in the frequently terrifying, accurate and unsettling film, The Exorcist, which, because of the way in which it portrayed demonic possession, is also Fr Amorth's favourite film.

Prayer to St Michael the Archangel

In the Name of the Father and of the Son and of the Holy Ghost. Amen.

Most glorious Prince of the Heavenly Armies, Saint Michael the Archangel, defend us in our battle against principalities and powers, against the rulers of this world of darkness, against the spirits of wickedness in the high places [Eph. 6, 12]. Come to the assistance of men whom God has created to His likeness and whom He has redeemed at a great price from the tyranny of the Devil. Holy Church venerates thee as her guardian and protector; to thee, the Lord has entrusted the souls of the redeemed to be led into Heaven. Pray therefore the God of Peace to crush Satan beneath our feet, that he may no longer retain men captive and do injury to the Church. Offer our prayers to the Most High, that without delay they may draw His mercy down upon us; take hold of "the dragon, the old serpent, which is the Devil and Satan", bind him and cast him into the bottomless pit "that he may no longer seduce the nations" [Rev. 20, 2-3].

The Exorcism

In the Name of Jesus Christ, our God and Lord, strengthened by the intercession of the Immaculate Virgin Mary, Mother of God, of Blessed Michael the Archangel, of the Blessed Apostles Peter and Paul and all the Saints **(and powerful in the holy authority of our ministry)**, we confidently undertake to repulse the attacks and deceits of the Devil.

(NOTE: Lay people using this injunction should omit the words marked out above in **bold script.**)

Psalm 67

God arises; His enemies are scattered and those who hate Him flee before Him. As smoke is driven away, so are they driven; as wax melts before the fire, so the wicked perish at the presence of God.

V. Behold the Cross of the Lord, flee bands of enemies.
R. The Lion of the tribe of Juda, the offspring of David, hath conquered.
V. May Thy mercy, Lord, descend upon us.
R. As great as our hope in Thee.

(The crosses in the following text indicate a blessing to be given if a priest recites the Exorcism. If a lay person recites it, they indicate the Sign of the Cross to be made silently by that person.)

We drive you from us, whoever you may be, unclean spirits, all Satanic powers, all infernal invaders, all wicked legions, assemblies and sects. In the Name and by the power of Our Lord Jesus Christ, ✠ may you be snatched away and driven from the Church of God and from the souls made to the image and likeness of God and redeemed by the Precious Blood of the Divine Lamb. ✠

Most cunning serpent, you shall no more dare to deceive the human race, persecute the Church, torment God's elect and sift them as wheat. ✠

The Most High God commands you. ✠

He with whom, in your great insolence, you still claim to be equal. "God who wants all men to be saved and to come to the knowledge of the truth" (I Tim. 2, 4). God the Father commands you. ✠

God the Son commands you. ✠

God the Holy Ghost commands you. ✠

Christ commands, God's Word made flesh, commands you . ✠

He who to save our race outdone through your envy, "humbled Himself, becoming obedient even unto death" (Phil. 2, 8); He who has built His Church on the firm rock and declared that the gates of Hell shall not prevail against Her, because He will dwell with Her "all days even to the end of the world" (Matt. 28, 20). The sacred Sign of the Cross commands you. ✠

As does also the power of the mysteries of the Christian faith. ✠

The glorious Mother of God, the Virgin Mary, commands you. ✠

She, who, by her humility and from the first moment of her Immaculate Conception, crushed your proud head. The faith of the holy Apostles, Peter and Paul, and of the other Apostles commands you. ✠

The blood of the Martyrs and the pious intercession of all the Saints command you. ✠

Thus, cursed dragon, and you, diabolical legions, we adjure you by the living God. ✠

By the true God. ✠

By the holy God. ✠

By the God who so loved the world that He gave up His only Son, that every soul believing in Him might not perish but have life everlasting" [St. John 3, 16]; stop deceiving human creatures and pouring out to them the poison of eternal damnation; stop harming the Church and hindering her liberty. Begone, Satan, inventor and master of all deceit, enemy of man's salvation. Give place to Christ in Whom you have found none of your works; give place to the One, Holy, Catholic and Apostolic Church acquired by Christ at the price of His Blood. Stoop beneath the all-powerful Hand of God; tremble and flee when we invoke the Holy and terrible Name of Jesus, this Name which causes Hell to tremble, this Name to which the Virtues, Powers and Dominations of Heaven are humbly submissive, this Name which the Cherubim and Seraphim praise unceasingly repeating: Holy, Holy, Holy is the Lord, the God of Hosts.

V. O Lord, hear my prayer.

R. And let my cry come unto Thee

V. May the Lord be with thee

R. And with thy spirit.

Let us pray.

God of Heaven, God of Earth, God of Angels, God of Archangels, God of Patriarchs, God of Prophets, God of Apostles, God of Martyrs, God of Confessors, God of Virgins, God who has power to give life after death and rest after work: because there is no other God than Thee and there can be no other, for Thou art the Creator of all things, visible and invisible, of Whose reign there shall be no end, we humbly prostrate ourselves before Thy glorious Majesty and we beseech Thee to deliver us by Thy power from all the tyranny of the infernal spirits, from their snares, their lies and their furious wickedness. Deign, O Lord, to grant us Thy powerful protection and to keep us safe and sound. We beseech Thee through Jesus Christ Our Lord.

Amen.

V. From the snares of the Devil,

R. Deliver us, O Lord.

V. That Thy Church may serve Thee in peace and liberty:

R. We beseech Thee to hear us.

V. That Thou may crush down all enemies of Thy Church

R. We beseech Thee to hear us.

Holy water is sprinkled in the place where we may be.

Before leaving the subject of Fr Amorth and his less than favourable views on the Masonic Order, we should look at the Freemasons. Although repeatedly stating that there is nothing remotely magickal about the Masonic Order or its degrees, it has some seriously magickal overtones in at least one of its rites. In the 18th Degree of the Ancient and Accepted Scottish Right of Freemasonry, we find: "Then as 'PHREE MESSEN' or 'children of light' they are instructed in methods of building a new temple without sound of hammer and when the spirit realizes that it is far from its heavenly home, a prodigal, feeding upon the unsatisfactory husks of the material world, that apart from the Father, it is 'Poor, naked and blind,' when it knocks at the door of a mystic temple like that of the Rosicrucians and asks for light, when it receives the desired instruction after due qualification by building and ethereal soul-body, a temple or house eternal in the heavens, not made with hands and without sound of hammer, when its nakedness is clothed with that house (see Cor. 4, 5) **then the neophyte receives 'The Word,' the open sesame to the inner worlds and learns to travel in foreign parts in the invisible worlds. There he takes soul-flights into heavenly region and qualifies for higher degrees under more direct instruction from The Grand Architect of The Universe, who fashioned both Heaven and Earth. There are 3x3 degrees in the lesser Mysteries; when the candidate has passed the 9th Arch, he is in the Holy of Holies, which forms the gate to greater fields beyond the scope of Masonry."** (my emphasis)

If this is not a clear description of a magickal ceremony, using a word of power to achieve ascendance over the laws of nature, then I don't know what is. So, perhaps, the indefatigable Fr Amorth may have some justification in what he says. Do not assume that I am attacking the Freemasons here, for I am not, but it does seem as if, in spite of their denials, at some of the higher degrees within the Masonic Order, it does operate at a genuinely magickal level and not in any speculative sense either.

Chapter 14
Malachi Martin

Before finally leaving the matter of exorcism, perhaps we should pause to look at the record of another exorcist, this time the widely-travelled former Roman Catholic priest, Fr Malachi Martin. On the face of it, Fr Martin (1921 – 1999), who was born in 1921 in County Kerry in Ireland and held dual Irish and American citizenship, was best known as a former Jesuit priest who performed exorcisms, many of them off his own back and often without the official sanction of the Catholic Church. His work in this field is graphically described in his best-selling personal factual account, *Hostage to the Devil: The Possession and Exorcism of Five Living Americans,* published in 1975, but the truth, as always, is rather different.

His background is impressive. He was a university-educated polyglot who spoke at least ten languages, including French, German, Russian, Chinese, Hebrew and Modern Arabic. He was also well-versed in such classical languages as Latin and Aramaic. He studied experimental psychology, anthropology and physics, all subjects that may have had some influence on his ideas about the reality of demonic possession. In addition to this, he was also an acknowledged expert on the Dead Sea Scrolls and published two books about the subject. It has to be said that, in some ways, he resembles the scholarly character of Fr Merrin, one of the two priests who officiated in the film, The Exorcist, and it has been suggested that Merrin's character was based upon him.

He was originally regarded as a liberal and progressive thinker, but following the profound changes made to Church doctrine during the Vatican II council, he became disillusioned by the reforms taking place, especially among his beloved Jesuits. Fr Martin had joined the Jesuit order aged thirty-three on the 15th of August, 1954, which was, incidentally, the Feast of the Assumption and the age at which Christ was crucified. In 1965, he requested permission to leave the order, a request granted personally by Pope Paul VI in June, 1965, but this was only from the strictures of poverty and obedience, and significantly not from celibacy, so he effectively remained an ordained but strictly secular priest. Pope Paul also requested him to exercise his considerable talents in the specialised fields of media and communications. When his book concerning exorcism was eventually published, it contained claims, in addition to the five that were highlighted, that he had assisted in many others, but a few years later, in 1996, the 'many' had expanded to actually performing thousands of them, both minor and major. In this, at least, his claims mirror those of Fr Amorth, which includes his increasing disenchantment with the loss of perceived prestige both for the Church and its priests.

This frustration found an outlet in another best-selling, non-fiction book that he released in 1987, entitled The Jesuits: The Society of Jesus and the Betrayal of the Roman Catholic Church. In this work, he vented his irritation about his much beloved order, accusing them of sundering the traditions of the Church and replacing them with communist ideas. This is actually no surprise and Fr Martin should, perhaps, have known better, because the Jesuits, although fervent upholders of Catholic Church dogma, have repeatedly had accusations levelled at them of being left-wing in their outlook as compared to the right-wing views of, for example, Opus Dei. Examples of this are widespread and when Jesuits were sent to tend to the needs of the masses, both in spiritual and secular matters in South American countries, they frequently 'went native' and openly opposed the various ruling authorities. The frequent abuse directed at Fr Martin has been aimed at the various (and serious) claims he made. These were not only about his role in the various exorcisms that propelled him into the public eye, but also at the considerably more serious allegations he made about the infiltration of Satanists (and others who seek to destroy the Catholic Church from within) into the Vatican. It has been suggested that much of this criticism originated from the hierarchy of the Jesuits who were far from happy about the publication of his factual book about them. The criticism continues even after his death.

Although he continued to work and travel widely in various capacities, the role of exorcist being one of them, there were hints that his status as a private individual might have been rather more than was obvious at first sight. It may even be possible that he was acting as some kind of intelligence gatherer/agent for conservative major players within the Holy See. His own conservatism verged on outspoken opposition to the changes driven through by Vatican II and he continued to say the Mass in Latin (the Tridentine Mass as originally approved by the Council of Trent). It was a few years before his death in 1999, from a brain haemorrhage, that some of his really worrying accusations were made. These were not subtle hints or vague innuendos, these were offered as blunt statements of fact.

A few years before Fr Martin died, he had a private meeting with Pope John Paul II (a debriefing and consultation, perhaps?) and he began work on what would probably have been his most provocative non-fiction work of all, entitled Primacy: How the Institutional Roman Catholic Church became a Creature of the New World Order. His motivation in pursuing this particular path is uncertain and whether he considered the New World Order both a reality and threat even more so, but if one considers that this organisation is accused of being a front for just about every force of evil, spiritual and otherwise, in this world and beyond, then his incentive becomes clear. What also becomes clear is that both Fr Martin and, indeed, at least one Pope believed that the influence of this organisation and the abomination it supposedly conceals was already present in the Vatican. In 1972, Pope Paul VI said, "Through some crack or other in the temple of God, the smoke of Satan has entered." This is a comment that today carries with it the taint of something unclean and the charges of the sexual abuse of children, something all too common in Satanic rituals, continues to emerge from what should be one of the holiest, most sacred and chaste locations on the planet.

Fr Martin also firmly believed that at least two popes were murdered. One, Pope Pius XI was assassinated on the orders of the Italian fascist dictator, Benito Mussolini, because of his outspoken criticism of the regime. He also alleged, through the literary device of his book, The Vatican: A Novel, that John Paul I was murdered on the orders of the KGB, assisted by Vatican insiders, which is actually something that has been frequently speculated about in various quarters. He goes on to suggest that the notorious 11th Century, Pope Benedict IX, was involved in Satanism and magick and that one of the principle architects of communism, Karl Marx, was also a Satanist and, given the enmity between the Catholic Church and the atheistic ideals at the core of communism, this really should be no great surprise. Fr Martin's mention of Pope Benedict IX is entirely justified and even the Catholic Encyclopaedia describes him as 'A disgrace to the chair of St Peter', while St Peter Damien describes his as "A demon from Hell disguised as a priest" and Pope Victor III talks about his "Rapes, murders, and other unspeakable acts". Given the inclinations of this pope, the charges of Satanism are probably richly deserved, so perhaps the talk of 'The smoke of Satan entering the Vatican' is something that has lengthy historical precedence.

The use of fiction to highlight his concerns about the Church has served Fr Martin well and, through the pages of his books, he has claimed that not only are devil worshipers actually present in the Vatican, but they conduct their magickal rituals and invocations there as well. He also accuses high-ranking members of the Curia, including the most senior of all at the time, Pope Paul IV, of being Freemasons. This charge was also laid against Pope John XXII, but again we should remember the scandals that surrounded the Vatican Bank, (the Banco Ambrosiano) and the existence of the Masonic Lodge called 'P2' or 'Propaganda Due'. This organisation had intimate associations with the Vatican and the subsequent death of lodge member, Roberto Calvi (the so called 'God's banker'), found hanged under Blackfriars Bridge in London. It was a death that bore many hallmarks of a ritual murder and displayed several examples of Masonic symbolism (not least its very location). The entire episode appears to suggest that the Vatican entered some kind of 'devil's pact' (perhaps literally) with the Masonic Order to maintain its position and influence in what is rapidly becoming a secular, western world.

Interestingly, though, while the influence of religion seems to be waning in the West, the same is not the case in Africa, where it grows and flourishes. This has created its own problems, especially with the emergence of the Zambian Archbishop Emmanuel Milingo, a priest with a similar outlook to that of Fr Martin. Fr Milingo, who was, eventually, stripped of his position as archbishop, is given to outspoken observations that the Vatican has been overrun by devil worshipers, who hold formal ceremonies, honouring their deity, within its walls. Fr Milingo attracted much criticism, not only from the Vatican, but in his native Zambia, as well, where other priests, formerly subservient to him, openly accused him of sorcery and witchcraft. The charge was made that his services, which involved practices similar to those seen in Pentecostal and Evangelical worship, owed more to traditional witchcraft than Catholicism.

While living in Italy, there were repeated tales of miraculous cures from cancer, AIDS and other ailments at church services he held and thousands regularly made their way to other ceremonies where he conducted mass exorcisms. The reaction from the Vatican came from the then Cardinal Joseph Ratzinger (now Pope Benedict XIV). An edict was issued specifically forbidding exorcisms and charismatic healing during Mass, although the Church obviously still recognises miraculous healing and the effectiveness of exorcism as a refuge of last resort. Former Archbishop Milingo has also written about his encounters with Satan and, at a conference in 2000, held at Fatima in Portugal, he again stated, categorically, that Satan was present within the Vatican and he is protected by those who rule there.

Two men with a very similar outlook making charges that, for obvious reasons, are fervently denied at all levels within the Catholic Church and every attempt is made to denigrate and smear those making them, but are the accusers correct? The truth is that it is nigh on impossible to penetrate the wall of official secrecy that surrounds the Vatican at all levels, especially that of doctrine. The only way that the truth will emerge is from those who feel so marginalized or outraged at what they find that they are prepared to endure the automatic rejection and personal odium that would follow such revelations. Even the laity would reject such charges and revelations and who can blame them, because, for the most part, their contact with the Church is through a local priest who is almost certainly not aware of what occurs at the highest levels. Yet, even here, there must be doubt, especially in view of the charges of the sexual abuse of children directed at some priests, is this evidence of Satanic influence or something else? The answer is that since, as we have seen, the Church, and indeed all religion, is founded on magickal precepts, then the suspicion will always remain that the charges have some basis in fact.

Chapter 15
The Vatican

Since it has been mentioned several times in the forgoing text, before continuing, we should consider the role of the Vatican in these matters, because its role as the spiritual heart of the Roman Catholic Church and repository of a wealth of occult knowledge is pivotal to what is contained in this book. For the sake of simplicity, every major organisation requires at least one recognisable base from which to operate and the Catholic Church is no different. From approximately 600AD until 1870, following series of territorial conquests orchestrated by the Kingdom of Piedmont–Sardinia, which ended with the defeat of Rome, the Catholic Church consolidated its outlying seats of power and amalgamated them in one location. The reigning Pope of the time, Pius IX, fully aware of the politics involved, decided that he had to establish a form of politically-neutral authority, so, from 1870 to 1929, the Pope and his successors closed the gates of the Vatican Palace and set themselves up as 'The Prisoners of Rome' and set about devising various forms of abuse to hurl at the secular Italian government, which was located a few hundred meters way in Rome itself.

As comparatively recently as 1922, when Benito Mussolini came to power with his fascists, he decided that the state of affairs between the Vatican and Rome was divisive and hinted to outsiders that the Church and State were not reading from the same page. This was especially important, since the country was essentially Catholic, as were many of members of Mussolini's government and the Catholic faith was a worldwide force, therefore, any perceived differences were damaging to the image of national unity that Mussolini wished to project. To overcome this, Mussolini sent an envoy to discuss an accommodation with Pope Pius, who was quick to see several advantages for the Church.

This resulted in the Lateran Treaty and the creation of an independent city-state, governed by the Pope as its supreme ruler (effectively its king and head of state) with the assistance of the Curia. The end result was the tiniest country in the world, which is much smaller than Andorra, Monaco or San Marino. However, for all its diminutive size, it wielded (and, indeed, continues to wield) a disproportionate amount power, not in any military sense, but in a much more insidious manner, because it can control how people think and act. Another gain for the Pope and the Church was a considerable sum, comprising both money and bonds from Mussolini's government to compensate for the loss of vast swathes of its land and properties and so it remains to this day and the Vatican is visited by tens of thousands of tourists and pilgrims each year.

One particular aspect of the Vatican that is not often discussed is the physical location of the vast conurbation that it has now become and this is typical of many ancient religious buildings. Among other things, the Basilica of St Peter, dedicated to the man appointed by Christ to found his Church and the very foundation of the Papacy, is built upon another ancient pagan site of worship, in this case, dedicated to the goddess, Cybele, who was one of the early Mother Goddesses and a possible template for the Virgin Mary. Another example of this, and still in Rome, is the presence of a temple to the sun god, Mithras, beneath the Basilica San Clemente, which is the oldest basilica in Rome. These are only two prime examples of how ancient pagan and occult traditions were literally engulfed by other emerging religious beliefs, especially the absorption of a sun god into their canon of teaching.

The tradition of sun worship is also found with the position taken by the Roman emperor, Constantine, who was absolutely central to the creation of the Christian Church when he convened the previously mentioned Council of Nicea. There are several reasons why this particular assembly was so important. One was that, prior to this, Jesus, although recognised as a great spiritual leader, was absolutely human, but after the council, He became divine and, therefore, an unassailable and magickal creation sent from God. During this council, another edict was passed, saying that belief in reincarnation, which had previously been an accepted part of the faith, was no longer allowed. Finally, the really interesting part of this was that Constantine, who had previously been a follower of Mithras, was described as "the light from the sun, who illuminates those furthest from him with his rays." This can easily be interpreted that, by extension, Constantine was regarded as a sun god in his own right and this would have been quite acceptable, since the Roman rulers were also seen as semi-divine beings anyway. In case anyone is in any doubt about the chronology of all this, prior to its adoption as the state religion of Rome, through the intervention of Constantine, there was no Roman Catholic Church, but there was a Christian Church which met in secret in an identical manner to the various mystery schools that flourished at the same time.

As an aside, this occult tradition is once again found in the actual positioning of churches and other places of worship. In many cases, although not all, churches are laid out on an east/west axis with the altar as the focal point at the east end. This is because it is intended to face the rising sun and also because Christ was traditionally crucified facing west, i.e. the setting sun. It serves the two-fold function of having the assembled congregation facing their dying god and, at the same time, seeing him symbolically reborn with the sunrise. Incidentally, as a further demonstration of just how deeply sun worship was integrated into Christian belief, early Christian burials dictated that the deceased should be buried with their feet facing east to await the resurrection. It is all couched in beautiful pagan symbolism and simplicity, of the dying and rising god, which, of course, symbolises the setting and rising sun. This can leave no-one in any doubt that all religions are based upon forgotten, fundamental truths of survival that have little or nothing to do with spirituality but, over time, have acquired this status. Returning to the alignment of places of worship, Rosslyn Chapel, near Edinburgh, is laid out in exactly this manner, with the added refinement of an ancient pentagonal 'light box' embedded high in the east wall above the circular Rose Window.

The 'light box', which is lined with the naturally reflective material, mica, contains a transparent red stone or crystal of some kind, designed to project a spot of red light into the chapel at sunrise on two days per year, which shows a clear understanding of the significance of the sun in mystical Christian belief. The same esoteric features are not found quite so often now because the design of churches is often left to the discretion of architects, who do not necessarily have any religious inclinations and whose instincts are for clean-cut functional design rather than enhancing any spiritual functions. The same thing happens in relation to the sonic properties of places of worship. As we saw previously, they were constructed to a set of ratios called the 'Golden Section' or 'Golden Mean', which was designed to enhance specific sounds and frequencies to exploit the power in them. Artists and painters used the same ratio as they composed their pictures, in order that they appeared harmonious to the eye, which was, of course, yet another reason why it was applied to sacred buildings. Again, we see an innate understanding of the untapped sources of magick around us that our forefathers accepted and understood and used for their benefit long before the establishment of formal religion

It is unlikely that this would have escaped the notice of the priests who worked and prayed in the churches built to these specifications and it must have been known to the fathers of the Catholic Church, who, in many cases, gave their specific permission for the construction of collegiate churches (like Rosslyn, whose original title was the Collegiate Church of St Matthew). Might this have been a case of using occult and magickal techniques in a manner that was approved because they were part of the fabric of a religious building? Based on this reasoning, it is fair to assume that the Church, in the beginning at least, was ambivalent toward some kinds of traditional magick, providing it exercised a degree of control over it and it suited their purpose. This appears in the so called 'Solfeggio Frequencies' found in Gregorian chants, where the sounds generated are thought to produce feelings of peace and understanding in both the singers and the audience. Naturally, the Church heartily approved of these and actively encouraged their use.

The Hidden Magick of Rosslyn Chapel

My own investigations into the esoteric functions of Rosslyn Chapel indicate that the church was designed to react in an utterly unique and magickal fashion to both sound and light in a bizarre example of what may even be a lost technology in action. The sound in question is a musical interval called an 'augmented fourth', which activates the 'secret' and later investigations indicated that a beam of light produced by sunlight shining on the previously mentioned red crystal, incorporated in the east wall of the chapel, may also be required. I consider myself privileged that the trustees of the chapel allowed me and a small number of colleagues to conduct a series of experiments there in both 1998 and 2005. What these experiments revealed is that the designers of the chapel, Sir William Sinclair and Sir Gilbert Hay, deliberately set out to incorporate a form of magick that would remain undetected by the Catholic Church authorities and this is not only having the Golden Mean incorporated into the construction of the chapel. We will look at this musical interval in more detail a little later.

I believe that what Sir William and Sir Gilbert did was to literally 'tune' the chapel to give a certain response to the combination of a specific musical note and red light. The fact that they went to such remarkable lengths to conceal their handiwork from the Church is not surprising. We should remember that the Sinclair family, although they were immensely rich and powerful, were not above the rules and regulations laid down by the Church and, because of this, could not risk being branded as heretics and, probably, magicians as well. Although the twin charges of heresy and excommunication carry little or no stigma nowadays, in Sir William's time, because of the instinctive belief in a Creator God as a given, they were extremely serious accusations indeed and could bring down the entire Sinclair and Hay families and lead to the forfeiture of their possessions. That said, it is even possible that Sir Gilbert did not realise what Sir William was trying to do and merely carried out his friend's directions, blissfully unaware of the magickal underpinnings.

It is known that Sir William had a great deal of sympathy for the unfair treatment meted out to the Knights Templar, following their proscription by King Philip le Bel of France, in collusion with Pope Innocent IV, and it may have been in a belated response to this that Sir William took the steps he did. Bear in mind that his grudge must have been hereditary, because the chapel was constructed almost 100 years after the official disbandment of the Templar Order. Researchers like Lomas and Knight, authors of the fascinating The Hiram Key and other works, have even suggested that the chapel was actually intended as a monument and shrine to the Templars and its use as a church was almost a by-product. Lomas and Knight even infer (with some justification) that the chapel is a copy of Herod's temple in Jerusalem, even to its location on the edge of the Esk Valley. The reason for the enmity between King Philip and the Templar Order appears to have been two-fold. One was the legitimate fear that the Templars, who, at the time, were probably the wealthiest and most powerful organisation in France, if not the whole of Europe, may have had the intention of creating their own independent state in the South of France, which would have presented an obvious and serious threat to the king.

The other reason was that, due to the costs of loans incurred from the Templars to finance various wars and to fund various domestic projects, the king owed the Order the equivalent of his entire treasury and, having squeezed his subjects almost dry through ever increasing taxation, could not pay it back. His initial tax raising measures were directed against the Jews, who finally tired of the continual and ruinous taxation and left France in their droves. He also realised that, if he could have the Templars removed from their unique position of effectively being above any civil law (they were answerable only to the papacy), at a stroke, he could cancel his debt and seize the Templar funds. To do this, he had to create a situation whereby the Pope would be forced to disown them and so he set about creating such a situation and the best way to do this was to have the Templars accused of heresy, something that not even the Pope could tolerate or condone.

To his credit, King Philip set about his task with considerable skill and gerrymandered and politicised the papacy until a pope of his choosing was installed as head of the Catholic Church and the Holy See. He also conferred with the more experienced members of his court to invent a set of charges to ensure that the Templars were deposed from their unique position in the hierarchy of the Church and State. The charges included Satanism, blasphemy, sodomy, teaching women to abort, idolatry and the worship of a head (sometimes referred to as a demon) called 'the Baphomet'. After approaching the Pope with this set of charges, the necessary approval to have the Templars arrested and their assets seized was obtained and, on Friday the 13th of October, 1309, the warrants were acted upon. In a series of raids on all Templar properties and preceptories in France, the majority of the Templars, including their Grand Master, Jacques de Molay, were arrested and jailed. Interestingly, there is evidence to suggest that, the previous night, a Templar fleet of eighteen ships sailed from the port of La Rochelle, presumably carrying the contents of the treasuries. Unfortunately, this has to be an assumption, because there is no real evidence regarding what they carried.

This leads to some questions, the Templar Order must have had spies and informers in the court of King Philip, and it is highly unlikely that they would not, so they would have known what was about to befall them. This being so, why did they fail to escape while they could? Although it is also possible that they did have prior knowledge, hence the conspicuous lack of booty in the various preceptory treasuries, after all, the king did not find the treasure he expected, so why did the Grand Master elect to remain? The answer to this may be sheer arrogance on the part of de Molay and his knights, assuming that their position alone would shield them from any sort of retribution. This oversight (or folly) ultimately proved to be the end of the Templar Order, in France at least, although it did continue for some time in various forms under different names in other countries, where they were positively welcomed and feted. Be that as it may, perhaps we should look at the charges themselves, since they closely match the practices attributed to the Black Mass and those who conducted it.

Satanism, blasphemy, sodomy, teaching women to abort, idolatry and the worship of a head called 'the Baphomet'. Since any one of these charges should have been enough to bring down the Templars, perhaps including a number of grave accusations was seen as kind of insurance to guarantee a conviction. Or is there something else afoot here? The clue may lie with the accusations that the Templars worshipped a head called 'The Baphomet'. This strange artefact has had many attributions laid against it. As already mentioned, it was claimed to be a demon, but, stranger still, it has also been claimed to be either the mummified head of Christ or, in other versions, the head of John the Baptist, although there are many other variants on this.

Actually, the claim that it is the head of the Baptist may carry slightly more weight, considering that there are no records that Christ was ever actually beheaded, but there is ample biblical evidence that John was decapitated. Of course, since the body of Christ was miraculously/magickally raised into Heaven on the third day after His death (or so we are told) there is no way of knowing. This astonishing event alone raises considerable speculation, but suffice it to say that it also prevented any difficult question being asked about His divinity. As a matter of interest, according to the Catholic Church, the Virgin Mary was evidently raised bodily into Heaven as well, something that did not pass into Church dogma until November, 1950, when Pope Pius XII, under the remit of papal infallibility, declared that this was the case and from then on it was accepted as another literal, if unlikely, 'truth'. Other variations on this have it that she ascended to Heaven forty days after her death, while yet other beliefs are certain that she ascended while still alive. All this, if true, is another magnificent example of powerful miraculous/magickal forces at work.

The Baphomet appears in various guises. In some accounts it is a human head and in others it is a Satanic, hermaphrodite goat. The goat interpretation was eagerly embraced by a number of occultists, most notably Aleister Crowley and Alphonse Louis Constant, better known as the mage Eliphas Levi, and more recently by, amongst others, Anton Szandor LaVey, founder and high priest of The Church of Satan. In this incarnation, especially in connection with Levi, it is sometimes referred to as the Goat of Mendes. Levi gives the following description of the Baphomet/goat:

* The head of a goat
* The upper body of a woman
* Cloven feet
* A pair of wings
* A candle on its head
* A symbol of revelation combining male potency and the four elements and intelligence

Although this image gained popular acceptance in the public psyche due to its passing similarity with the gargoyles found on the rooves of Templar preceptories, it is not necessarily accurate. The nearest contemporary image depicting the Sabbatic Goat of Mendes is found in a painting by Francisco Goya, who, in 1800, painted The Witches Sabbat, which shows a group of women offering their children to a seated goat. Yet another variant on the word, Baphomet, suggests that it can be interpreted as meaning 'Sophia' the Greek word for wisdom. This certainly appears to corroborate two alternate interpretations. Levi stated that Baphomet is comprised of the abbreviations 'Temp Ohp Ab' that are rooted in the Latin, 'Templi omnium hominum pacis abhas' meaning 'The father of universal peace among men'.

On the other hand, the word may originate from the Arabic 'Abu-fihamat' or 'father of understanding'. Finally, Anton La Vey and his Church of Satan claimed that 'Baphomet' was their identifying symbol, normally surrounded by five Hebrew letters, spelling LNYThN or 'Leviathan', one of the Lords of Hell. On the other hand, alternative reports of this object describe it as either a skull or having skull-like qualities and having the feeling of smoothness or, yet again, as having a beard. Of all the available descriptions, the reference to a head seems the more credible and is supported, to some extent, by the confessions extracted from the captured Templars. As one would imagine, these confessions were extracted under torture, but unless those undergoing this torment were deliberately coached in what to say or the confessions were prewritten and only required signing, assuming the victims still were able to do so, the descriptions of the Baphomet appear to match one another.

So the Templars may have been involved in magickal ceremonies of one kind or another and, when added to long standing speculation that Sir William Sinclair may have been involved in High Magick, there is some evidence to suggest that one of the several secrets allegedly hidden inside Rosslyn Chapel is the very same Baphomet. Of course, the lost treasure of the Templars and even the treasure of Solomon's Temple are reputedly there as well. There is also a connection concerning the relationship of the Templars with the sun god interpretation of Christ. While the use of sun imagery in Catholic Church doctrine is an uneasy one at best and would obviously be denied, nevertheless, it may still be valid and it is still used within at least one branch of modern day Templarism, the 'Militi Templi Scotia', or Scottish

Knights Templar (which, as with the Masonic Templar degrees, is not in any way related to the Catholic Church).

This is found in the higher degrees of this order where a crucifix emblazoned by the head of Christ set in a golden sunburst is used. There is also another version of this where a crucifix with the head of Apollo, again set in a sunburst is also used, implying a clear similarity between the two deities. At any rate, there is some evidence that, treasure or not, a secret is hidden in Rosslyn and my own research indicates that, as already mentioned, it might be possible to unlock it through the use of a specific sound combined with light. The sound, an augmented fourth, is the main key, so let's look at this in some detail, as it, once again, involves the Church. In medieval times, the Church issued a decree, stating that it would not tolerate the use of augmented fourths in Church music, even going as far as to call this musical interval the 'Diabolus in Musica' or 'The Devil in Music', better known as the rather sinister sounding 'The Devil's Chord'.

This is worth another short aside to look at the reasons behind the banning of The Devil's Chord in medieval Church music. When first introduced, it was allowed on the grounds that the concept of the Devil and the depiction of evil was fair play, but the Church authorities failed to appreciate that doing so using sound caused unease and disquiet in the listener. Since this musical interval, which is actually a 'tritone' spanning C to F#, appeared to produce the required impressions, it was adopted and used. However, apparently on 'technical grounds' (supposedly because it was too jarring and discordant), its use was later explicitly forbidden throughout the whole of Europe. One is tempted to ask why. Was this the only reason, because the screams and wails of those tortured during the cruelty of the Inquisition were also discordant and inharmonious, but apparently acceptable? There is some evidence that, through the deliberate design and ratio of many church buildings (the Golden Mean), this particular chord was having an unintended influence on a few susceptible members of the assembled congregations. The manner in how this secret was rediscovered is discussed in great detail and also the experiments related to the discovery are set out in the books, Rosslyn: Between Two Worlds and also in the Hole in the Sky. See sources and references at the end of the book.

Other Magickal Uses for Sound

It is now thought that if used in an appropriate location (e.g. a church built to a specific set of ratios), the chord created a sense of 'out of body experience' and altered states of consciousness in some of the faithful in much the same manner that rhythmic drumming and sound induces identical effects in shamanic cultures, where its use is widespread and encouraged. In these altered states, it is entirely conceivable that those so affected were, in effect, experiencing some kind of a mystical epiphany that the Church had no part in or, at least, not intentionally. Perhaps the individual was actually 'seeing God' or some of the other entities that inhabit the world that exists outside our standard level of consciousness and, if nothing else, the experience would be personal, intense and profoundly moving.

This would obviously be regarded as a 'bad thing' by the Church because (A) the contact was unapproved by them, (B) it was possible that the person having the experience might see their own way to enlightenment, (C) it might lead to a loosening of their power over the population or (D) to be generous, they might have had genuine concerns for the spiritual well-being of their flock. Once again, we must consider the mystical experiences of various monks, nuns and others who have attached themselves to the mainstream body of the Church. Their experiences were considered as automatically blessed because they passed some criteria set by the Church and the individuals who displayed these magickal phenomena were spiritually uplifted and did not suffer any obvious harm.

This is an important distinction between magickal manifestations and miraculous manifestations (and, of course, cures), which, once again, opens up a semantic minefield. If cures directly attributed to religious intervention are deemed miraculous, then why are all cures alleged to have been spiritually induced not considered miraculous? Surely all cures brought about by apparently spiritual and divine intervention are, by definition, miraculous? The answer to this, of course, comes from the assertion that cures (or healing) not obviously achieved by divine input may be demonically inspired. We are reminded that Satan can also perform miracles to suit his own ends and confuse the unwary. This is exactly the same set of values against which all manifestations of religious ecstasy are judged. If the demonstration, irrespective of what it is, for example stigmata, bi-location, prophecy, levitation etc., is accompanied with visions of God or His saints, then it is deemed miraculous. Conversely, if the manifestation leaves the person ill or shaken, then it is deemed demonic. This is still one of the litmus tests enshrined in the Catholic Church's process to define divinely inspired events or phenomena. All of this ties back into the mantra of approved and unapproved magickal events that were and still are being stage-managed by the Church for its own benefit.

It is interesting to note, however, that the deliberate use and exploitation of musical notes and frequencies was not the sole invention of the Roman Church and has been in use for millennia, especially by the priests and others, almost certainly shamans by any other name, who sought to commune with the invisible world of magick. There are several examples of this and, indeed, it is claimed by some that one of the notes in the Devil's Chord/tritone, in this case F# or 16Hz, is the natural harmonic of the planet and is the internal resonant frequency of the Great Pyramid. F# is also the tone to which

shamans from various countries and traditions tune their flutes. The
deliberate use of frequencies has also been noted in such structures as the
large megalithic burial cairn at Newgrange in Ireland, where a standing
frequency of 110Hz has been measured in the long passageway leading into
the centre of the cairn. It is unlikely that this was an accident because similar
effects have been noted at such ancient structures as Waylands Smithy in
Berkshire, England, and at Maes Howe, another ancient burial chamber
located on the Orkney Islands, off the coast of northern Scotland.

One can almost picture the scene (bearing in mind that, in these cases, the
use of the phenomenon was deliberate and encouraged): The mourners
and/or shamans and worshippers standing in line in the passage or grouped
together in a chamber, lit only by the guttering light of primitive oil lamps.
There is chanting and drums are beaten in a steady rhythm. The sounds are
modified and enhanced by the unusual acoustics of the enclosure. It is likely
that those in attendance would already be in a suggestible and expectant state
anyway and may even have taken some sort of mild, natural hallucinogen,
because this was part of their process of contacting the 'other side'. It can be
almost guaranteed that many of those present could and would have out of
body experiences, the crucial difference being that this was regarded as a
positive outcome and not something to be banned or denied. This is, at least,
honest and probably, to some extent, successful and it is partly why the Celts
and other early cultures learned to worship the unseen as well as the physical
world.

This brings us back to Rosslyn Chapel, where the magickal interfaces with
the physical and may be the reason why Sir William went to such lengths to
create what is still regarded as an enigma built in stone. I believe this is one
instance where the Church did not realise what he had done, otherwise they
would have stopped it and only now is that lost secret beginning to emerge.
In my opinion, Sir William created (by whatever means, but, possibly, some
forgotten magickal attributes of design and location) a kind of portal in the
north-east part of the chapel, right in front of the St Matthew altar, and this
portal conceals the path to some immense truth that was placed there to keep
it safe from the eyes of the profane and ignorant. What this truth is and what
it means, I have no idea, but the method of opening the portal (sound and
light) is, I believe, also encoded into the fabric of the chapel in the form of
the designs on the faces of the cubes in the ceiling of the retro-choir, where
the portal in located. So far, the portal has not been opened and, perhaps,
never will be, so, for the time being, the secret is safe. This is surely a
manifestation of magick at its most dramatic and successful and all brought
about by sound and frequency, two of the vital touchstones of this lost science.

Rock'n'Magick
Before leaving the association between music and magick, the evolution of

this relationship still continues, but in a much darker mode. I refer to the ongoing connection between 'heavy metal' music (a term coined by the writer, William Burroughs) and Satanism. Concern for the moral and spiritual welfare of the young, lest they should actually enjoy themselves, became a subject of deep concern for various groups of fundamentalist and evangelical Christians, especially in the USA. These groups have steadfastly condemned and damned rock music, which served as the springboard for heavy metal and its more dissolute and louder siblings, such as 'thrash metal', 'black metal' and 'death metal', almost since its inception. The reasons behind their attitude are based on the early blues music, from which rock music and its derivatives drew their inspiration. Another cause for their knee-jerk antipathy may even have connections with racism and the simple fact that the originators of the blues were the descendants of the black slaves who were kidnapped from the African continent to labour in the cotton plantations of the American Deep South. It should be added that these unfortunate people ended up in various western countries, including Britain, although, in general, they were treated with marginally better care.

The theory went that since they came from far away, heathen countries that did not share the 'civilised' Christian values of the West, they were, therefore, godless and worshipped strange idols and deities. Because of this, they were looked upon as little better than animals and were treated accordingly. This, of course, went for their spiritual values and beliefs as well. The grim hangover from these days found various outlets in the excesses of the Ku Klux Klan and other quasi-religious, racist organisations, although their activities have been greatly marginalized in more recent times, but still the music that developed to express the tribulations suffered by tens of thousands of slaves served as a convenient focus for the continued marginalizing of the people and their culture.

As the music born of despair was gradually assimilated into the culture of the 20th Century, almost by a process of osmosis, it began to influence the music favoured by young, white people, first in America and then the rest of the western world. Eventually, it was fused with other musical genres, into rock and roll or, perhaps, more accurately, 'beat music', because this definition may be more significant than it first appears. The reason that it achieved such a prominence in the culture of the West, especially among the young, was that it symbolised rebellion and angst, something that has been the trademark of youth almost since civilization began. As well as the groundswell of Christian indignation that grew in proportion to the influence of the devilish rock music in the USA, there were also similar cries of outrage in the Britain.

In 1956, an English Pentecostal minister averred that rock and roll would turn young people into devil worshippers and cause them to express themselves through sexual indulgence, adding that it would impair nervous stability and undermine the sanctity of marriage: a stern warning indeed. In the same year, the British newspaper, The Daily Mail, a publication that is traditionally phobic about anything that threatens the conservative status quo, or is perceived as, in some way, 'anti-English', stated that, "It is tribal, it is despicable and it is from America. It follows ragtime, blues, Dixie, jazz, hot cha cha and boogie-woogie, which surely originated in the jungle. We sometimes wonder if it is the Negro's revenge." Even although offensive and a product of a less liberal era, it is still unintentionally amusing in its Union Jack-waving bluster and xenophobia. It did, however, hint at one of the attributes of music (of any kind) to alter mood and even awareness. Some thirty years, later a Canadian psychologist noted that, "Rock has an incessant, driving beat, the same beat that people in primitive cultures use in their demonic rites and dances. If the beat is monotonous, it can induce a state of hypnosis."

The truth is that the psychologist is absolutely correct in his observations and, apart from the inclusion of the term, 'demonic', that is exactly what these so-called 'primitive cultures' do, simply because it facilitates their desire for contact with the divine and magickal. To some extent, the use of rhythms and frequency is deliberately exploited in discothèques to create and alter moods, although not necessarily to the point of altering consciousness. The rhythms used are measured in BPM (or 'beats per minute') and are often adjusted as the evening progresses. It is one of the features of 'trance music' and the frequently soporific moods that are induced using this kind of technique. The main reason that Satanism and black magick became associated with rock music as typified by such bands as AC/DC, Black Sabbath, Venom, Bathory, Led Zeppelin and even The Rolling Stones through their classic track, Sympathy For the Devil, was due to the rejection of conformity and the perceived 'freedom' that following beliefs like these could bring. It was seen that people like Aleister Crowley and Anton le Vey were in the vanguard of the counterculture and what they said – and, more importantly, did - was a template to be emulated and, if possible, improved on. This was, perhaps, a natural progression of the cultural upheaval and sexual liberation of the 1960s and '70s, when convention became something to be flouted and the use of recreational drugs became widespread (if not exactly legal).

As a reflection on the search for insidious, Satanic influences in individual tracks on albums, there were claims involving such covert techniques as 'subliminal advertising' and 'back masking'. Subliminal advertising has a long and chequered history that originates in the 1960s, where, as an experiment, extremely short clips of images or text were inserted into mainstream films to covertly encourage cinema (or even possibly TV) audiences to, for example, buy soft drinks or popcorn or anything else being promoted. It was calculated that, because of the short duration of the clips, they would not be consciously registered, but the subconscious mind would react to the stimulus and prompt the individual to comply with whatever suggestion was being made. However, their effectiveness was inconclusive and so the process did not proceed. This is just as well, because, quite apart from dubious ethical and moral considerations, if it had been successful, it is almost certain the technique would have been used worldwide for political and propaganda purposes, in effect, a type of mind control. A technique similar to subliminal advertising was actually used at least twice to good effect in the making of the previously mentioned, seminal film, The Exorcist.

The other technique of 'back masking' supposedly involved having the lyrics of songs contain certain messages that could only be discerned by playing the specific track backwards. Bands such as Judas Priest (or perhaps their record company) were accused of doing this. In fact, Judas Priest was specifically blamed for the deaths of two teenagers who killed themselves after listening to albums recorded by the band. The case was heard in 1990, but the accusations were dismissed. The results of back masking are dubious and can be likened to 'Electronic Voice Phenomenon' or EVP. In this technique, messages from the dead are allegedly picked up on tape recordings made at haunted locations. Sometimes the messages are heard apparently responding to questions asked by those present. However, it has to be said that, although they might be legitimate messages, in many cases (but not all), one has to be told what to listen for, otherwise the 'message' is indistinguishable from naturally-occurring background hiss and static.

The above mentioned bands used lyrics that, in some cases, mentioned certain magickal practices, although it is unlikely that many of the band members actually became involved in magickal ritual to any great depth. That said, it is widely believed that Jimmy Page, the lead guitar player of Led Zeppelin, who was an avowed Crowleyphile, did become involved in at least some of the magickal practices created by Aleister Crowley and, for some years, was the owner of one of Crowley's former abodes, Boleskine House, on the shores of Loch Ness, although it is not known if he ever lived there for any length of time. It is also not known if he still involves himself with these former interests. As for the rest, although they all seem to have drifted around in the magickal subculture to one degree or another, this was more likely to have been as voyeurs and dilettantes rather than active participants.

It is far from certain why music, like the aforementioned 'black metal' and 'death metal', attained the fragmented, but loyal, popularity that they did and also why this type of music became particularly popular in Scandinavia and in Norway in particular. Perhaps it struck resonant chords with the Viking berserker traditions in the Norwegian psyche, because the bands certainly adopted this imagery in their style of dress, a trend that, somehow, ended up with the use of Satanic imagery, Nazi emblems and uniforms used in the stage acts. One of the Norwegian acts, named Dimmu Borgir (a reference to the

Norwegian name for the entrance to Hell), although conforming to most of the 'black metal' traits, found itself pushed to the outer edges of the cult for not being evil enough. Conversely, perhaps this was why they made quite a lot of money in the process, something that put them even further beyond the pale of youthful rebellion and angst.

Chapter 16
The Process Church of the Final Judgement

Another aspect of the uneasy accommodations reached between magick and the New Age is found in the doctrines of the Process Church and is an example of cult-related ideas falling somewhere between the cracks of what passes for religion in the rarefied world of cults, yet still shares most of the tenets of cult practice. Such an organisation was embodied in the Scientology spin-off, 'The Process Church of the Final Judgement'. This bizarre organisation emerged in 1963 from a therapy group called 'Compulsions Analysis', founded by Robert Moore and Mary Anne McLean. Both were from quite different backgrounds and only met through their shared interest in Scientology. Following the old adage of opposites attracting, perhaps it was these differences that drew them together when they entered the intense training, therapy and considerable expense required to become Scientology practitioners.

Their feelings for one another grew and they married, then, becoming disenchanted with, as they saw it, the 'orthodoxy' of Scientology, they left to found their own therapy group. Shortly after this, perhaps for reasons of pragmatism, they changed their names to the distinctly exotic-sounding de Grimston. Their group quickly gained a following and it was from this kernel that a system called 'The Process' developed. The intensive conditioning sessions created an internally-charged atmosphere, whereby the group became totally absorbed in both the therapy and each other, thereby creating distrust and rejection of those on the outside. In effect, they were no longer restricted to behaviour acceptable to society in general and were also free to develop in any way they saw fit. This eventually encompassed the use of the darker aspects of the Christian religion. It also led to the cult adopting imposing uniforms, consisting of black cloaks adorned with goats heads and crucifixes, for their rites and meditations.

In June, 1966, the group left London and moved to the Bahamas, but eventually settled at Xtul on the Yucatan Peninsula. After they spent some time there, the parents of three group members attempted to rescue them from the clutches of the de Grimstons, causing the group to uproot once more and return to England, this time as a religion rather than a therapy group. During the next few years, the group expanded and set up chapters in Paris, Amsterdam, New York, Rome and Munich. However, in 1968, financial difficulties arose and Robert de Grimston sent some of his followers to obtain money by, in effect, begging. He supported this decision by the typically cynical use of scripture, in this case Matthew Chapter 10: "Take no money, for the individual [i.e. the Prosessean] has no need of it for himself. For our spiritual needs will be met by those to whom we give spiritually."

Here we have a prime example of twisting (or reinterpreting) scripture, in this case, to suit the needs of de Grimston and his acquisitive nature. In 1968, the group finally settled in America, establishing more chapters in Boston, Chicago and New Orleans. It was at this time that Robert and Mary Ann separated from the rest of the group and bestowed themselves with the title, 'The Omega'. This neatly conferred a notion of elitism upon them that bolstered their own ideas and self-image and made them an object of veneration for their followers. It was also a unique position to which their acolytes could not aspire. Presumably, the use of the term, 'The Omega', inferred that they were, indeed, the end product of the process, insofar as they represented the acme of perfection.

Although the methods of therapy practiced by the group became known as 'processes', hence the name of the church, their beliefs became ever more bizarre. Once again, in line with the Cathari and Bogomils etc., we see clear parallels with dualist and gnostic belief systems. Process doctrine stated that four Gods were created at the beginning of time, Jehovah was a wrathful god of vengeance and retribution, Lucifer (the light bringer) was fun loving, kind and valued success and peace. Satan, on the other hand, instilled two qualities in his followers. One was the desire to attain transcendence above the human realm and concentrate on achieving spiritual perfection. The other (and equal quality promoted) was a need to move outside one's humanity and human values and become obsessed with violence and excessive physical indulgence. The fourth element in this was Christ, who was seen as the link between the Gods and humanity.

The Gods were organised into sets of opposites, Jehovah and Lucifer, Christ and Satan, which characterised basic personality types and people desiring to learn their particular pattern could fill in a questionnaire. This, when used in conjunction with a device called a 'P Scope', would uncover unconscious feelings and ideas as interpreted by a process counsellor. The P-Scope, along with the individual degrees or 'processes' leading to enlightenment, is a further example of the groups' Scientologist roots. The P-Scope is an exact mirror of the 'E-meter' used in Scientology and serves exactly the same function, i.e. it measured galvanic skin response to a series of questions. It is also nothing particularly new and is a standard technique frequently employed by conventional psychologists in the treatment of stress-related conditions. These concepts and methods are virtually identical to those employed by the Scientologists, presumably achieving the same, highly subjective rate of success. Although The Process Church no longer operates under that name, there are three other groups that appear to have incorporated at least some of the original theology in their own beliefs. They are, 'The Society of Processeans', the 'Foundation Faith of God' and 'The Terran Order'. Although little is known about this last group, it is similar to the science-fiction origins of Hubbard's original Scientologists.

While the above account is by no means exhaustive, it does give a flavour of the more extreme beliefs currently in existence. It is clear that cult members are a very special breed of person in search of something that conventional scripture-based belief cannot supply. To the rational mind, it seems incredible that anyone could believe the dire, doom laden and extreme sermons delivered by the misguided, unscrupulous and, in many cases, barking mad leaders of these movements, but, unfortunately, people are not rational beings. It is certain that, as with groups dedicated to magickal practices, they become socially isolated. Many of these cults are highly demanding and develop effective, internal support mechanisms out of necessity, in effect, creating their own exclusive social reality. This is known as 'Social Implosion' and occurs when the groups' own internal structures strengthen sufficiently to permit the eventual replacement of external structures. When these groups are isolated or enclosed and external news and opinions tightly controlled or, indeed, completely absent, the group paradigm, irrespective of how irrational it is, becomes the truth absolute, which, when coupled to the charisma and teachings of a leader, usually a concoction of truth, lies, magickal techniques and speculation, it can become a heady and dangerous mixture.

The exaggerated, unquestioning and distorted view of reality is vital to sustain them and their beliefs. Cult leaders all appear to have specific personality traits: they are charismatic, domineering, imposing and glib, see others as inferior, have a drive for power and authority, are hostile to criticism and tend to paranoia, a trait also common in despots and tyrants. However, in addition to the negative traits, many of these cult leaders also claimed to have miraculous and/or magickal powers and abilities, which, as in the case of Jim Jones and his ultimately doomed 'People's Temple', included the claimed ability to heal the sick and raise the dead. It was the rule rather than the exception that the leaders were perceived to have a direct line to God, through which they received their increasingly bizarre prophecies and messages. What these messages actually were may also serve as a guide to their source, which was not necessarily the troubled subconscious mind of the self-styled prophet.

Ultimately, providing a specific belief system, magickal or otherwise, does not set out to deliberately harm or abuse its members (or those outside it), it is relatively harmless. However, when the weak or vulnerable are coerced, gulled or browbeaten into accepting a harmful or dangerous doctrine, then it may be fair and reasonable for external forces to intervene and save them from themselves. While this course of action may not please those who believe (personal choice and freedom should not be infringed for any reason), it is sometimes necessary to protect the innocent and, sometimes, the merely gullible. While it is easy to automatically assume that an individual is too independent or strong-willed to become enmeshed in the fevered world of magickal cults, bear in mind the methods employed by high-pressure salesmen, so-called 'motivational speakers' and charismatic religious evangelists. They use every psychological trick in the book to convince the customer or audience member that they need whatever service, life-style gadget or magickal 'holy item' they are selling. It you have ever attended a time-share presentation (or watched one of the God salesmen at work, described elsewhere in this book) you will recognise exactly how this done.

The techniques described here are used to condition members of many quasi-religious and magickal cults, although they have very obvious downsides and can be extremely risky for the mental well-being of the cult members. On the other hand, they do have a positive side, if used to gauge levels of magickal indoctrination. As we have seen, the concept of Chaos Magick is predicated on the ability of the magician to exclude all external and irrelevant thoughts other than the spell he or she is attempting to operate. It is also fair to say that the more people who believe a specific outcome will result from a specific action or wish then the more likely it is to happen. Therefore, when looked at from that perspective, the people held within the bonds of a cult are likely to be susceptible to manipulation in any magickal enterprise. In fact, the same might be said for a church congregation while at prayer, if the prayer is being used as a combined offering and request to create a change in the nature of reality.

As a final observation on the extremist uses of religion, we still see this today in the violent and disproportionate reaction of certain Muslims to any perceived slight against the Islamic faith and it is most often observed in backward, Third World countries. Therefore, perhaps the roots lie in the fact that the populations of these countries have nothing else in their lives that could be regarded as having any real value. In the absence of material possessions, the lure of a nebulous, but glorious, reward in the afterlife assumes a vitally important place in their, otherwise, empty lives, to the point of hysteria and obsession. This social paradigm, which is based on fear and, to some extent, desperation, gradually died out in the West following the late Middle Ages, when education slowly began to permeate throughout society.

Chapter 17
The Magickal Court

As already mentioned, the Court of King Louis XIV was a hotbed of intrigue as the nobles and favourites jockeyed for position and rank in the pecking order and, as it transpired, this led to the discovery of some of the most horrifying instances of black magick and devil worship ever known. This involved a series of horrific rituals instigated by Francois-Athenais, the Marquise de Montespan, a beautiful young woman who was a member of the queen's retinue and also the king's mistress, to retain her favoured place in the hierarchy of the court. The gossip surrounding the machinations of de Montespan and her associates uncovered another major scandal called the 'Affair of the Poisons'. All of this came about as a direct result of the continuous pressure within the court circle to create, maintain, then defend the social standing of individual courtiers. The outrages began with an inexplicable series of deaths among the aristocracy and ended with charges of murder, poisoning and witchcraft being directed at the inner circle surrounding the king himself. The king, fully appreciating his own position, was understandably concerned and, to safeguard himself, he appointed some unfortunate servants as food tasters.

The scandal began in 1675 when the Marquise de Brinvilliers and her lover and accomplice, an army officer called Godin Sainte de Croix, were tried for the 1666 poisoning of her father and brothers. The Marquise was also suspected of poisoning the patients in a hospital she regularly visited in a charitable capacity. The rumour was that she had tested the effectiveness of the poisons on the luckless inmates. She fled, but was arrested in Liege and made to confess using the so called 'water cure', which involved inserting a funnel into the throat and forcing the person involved to consume up to sixteen consecutive pints of water while bent backwards over a frame. Sometimes this procedure was refined by inserting a thin strip of felt into the throat to induce gagging and choking as well. Her actual execution involved beheading and the corpse was finally burned at the stake. Her accomplice died in prison of natural causes.

During her interrogation, the Marquise had helpfully provided the names of others who were purchasing poisons and, based on these revelations, the authorities arrested a number of alchemists and clairvoyants on suspicion of selling and providing aphrodisiacs, séances and the quaintly named 'inheritance powders' (more commonly known as poison). When arrested, the accused were also encouraged to talk and, not surprisingly, supplied a lengthy list of patrons who had used their services to dispose of family members or rivals at court. One of the most notorious of those questioned was a midwife and witch (these unfortunate women were frequently regarded as one and the same thing) named Catherine Deshayes Monvoisin, better known simply as 'La Voisin'. The woman had been married to an unsuccessful businessman and tried to contribute to the family coffers, initially by prostitution then by palm reading and other forms of divination.

As her fame grew, she began to dabble in witchcraft and she, along with two accomplices, began supplying aphrodisiacs and poisons as well. One of these accomplices was a magician calling himself Lesage and the other was a defrocked priest named Etienne Guibourg. Among the unlikely ingredients employed by La Voisin in her potions and salves were toad bones, powdered moles teeth, iron filings, human blood and mummy dust. The use of mummy dust was considered as a kind of universal panacea for a number of medical conditions and there was a brisk trade between Egypt and Europe in mummies, so much so that the Egyptian authorities were forced to take action to stop it. It should be noted that the use and development of poisons was something of a growth industry during that era.

At the instigation of the king, acting through the chief of police, an officer called de Reynie, a special court called Chambre Ardente or 'Burning Court' was established and this group investigated many cases of alleged poisoning and witchcraft, especially those with links to the inner circle of the king. During the time of its existence (approximately five years - it was finally abolished in 1682) the court found thirty-four people guilty and sentenced them to death, not counting two who died under torture. The abolition of this special court came about mainly because the king grew increasingly uneasy about the bad publicity it created, quite apart from the implication that he was unable to control his own court. It did, however, indicate the seriousness of the crimes while providing a measure of protection for those involved and, undoubtedly, many were spared the humiliation and embarrassment of a trial because of their rank and the very nature of the crime.

During the interrogation of La Voisin, which was conducted by keeping her permanently drunk, surely a precursor of so called 'truth serums', not surprisingly, she implicated a number of people, but especially a former priest and accomplice, the obese and ill-favoured Abbé Étienne Guibourg, who was accused of officiating at many Black Masses. As we have seen previously, just because a priest has been defrocked (i.e. excommunicated and forbidden to say the Mass or participate in any Church-approved ceremonies) it does not mean that they are any less a priest with all the esoteric knowledge that entails. It was the details of these Black Masses that particularly nauseated the public, because, in addition to the worst forms of blasphemy, they also involved the ritual murder, torture and disembowelment of babies and children. It has been stated that, when a search was carried out of the garden surrounding La Voison's house, the remains of anything between 200 and 2,500 bodies of mutilated children were found. Whether or not this number of bodies actually was discovered is a moot point, since there are several conflicting reports, but it is reasonable to assume that there was no smoke without fire.

La Voisin stated that de Montespan had actively and willingly participated in the Black Masses along with the abbé Guibourg with the intention of retaining the affections of the king and that she had allowed her own naked body to be substituted for the altar. These Masses took the form of repeating a series of invocations, usually parodies of the Catholic Mass, the use of a desecrated host and offerings of human blood sacrifice in the form of children. The methods used to extract these confessions were on similar lines to those used during the Inquisition, therefore, anything that did emerge must be regarded with some suspicion, although, in general, there was a thread of consistency that did permeate what was said. In addition, it has also been suggested that the king sent agents to infiltrate some of the magickal groups and the accounts torn from those who were accused matched the reports supplied by his spies.

Chapter 18
Augustus Montague Summers

Much has been said about the barbaric excesses of the medieval inquisitors and rightly so, but less is known about those who chose to condemn magick (and witchcraft) in the most graphic terms in more recent and, presumably, enlightened times. Only the fact that we no longer live trapped in a morass of superstition, ignorance and fear (plus, of course, a much more enlightened legal system) prevented them from inciting new witch-hunts with their attendant hysteria, fear and butchery. Nevertheless, a few of these malicious zealots still were around and one such man was Augustus Montague Summers. He was born in April, 1880, the youngest of seven children of a prosperous banking family in Bristol, England. His early schooling was unremarkable, but he went on to study theology at the prestigious Trinity College, located in Cambridge, with the intention of becoming a priest in the Church of England.

He continued his training at Lichfield College and, in 1908, achieved the minor rank of deacon in the Anglican Church. He did not receive any further promotions in the church, which may have been due to his interest in Satanism. His interest in the subject and actually practicing it were two entirely different things and should have been no impediment, but the rumours of his alleged interest in young boys certainly was. He was tried on charges of this nature, but was eventually found not guilty and acquitted. That said, his first published work in 1907, Antinous, dealt with the disgusting and debased subject of pederasty. It seems strange that it is only now that effective legislation is in place to prevent any of these perverts having any contact with children.

Perhaps it reflected the hypocritical values of his times where many things were swept under the carpet to maintain the public façade of religious respectability and decency. Unfortunately, it is also something that still bedevils the Catholic Church to this day and has been highlighted by, at the time of writing, the evidence of an ongoing cover-up by the Church in Ireland during the late 20th Century, when it evidently put its own reputation before the interests of children abused by its priests in that country. The severity of the issue also forced Pope Benedict XIV to issue a letter of public apology.

In 1909, Summers converted to Roman Catholicism and began to adopt the garb and manner of a priest in that religion, which, given his theological training and the similarity between the two faiths, would have been relatively easy. It is here that we should look more closely at his actions, because there is considerably more to this than meets the eye. Yes, he did convert to Catholicism and adopted the extravagant soubriquet of Father Alphonsus Jesus-Mary Augustus Montague Summers, but this conversion was not in the mainstream Catholic Church, this was a schism called 'The Old Catholic Church'. Tellingly, among its differences with the Catholic Church is its acceptance of homosexuality as an acceptable lifestyle, which, at that time, was almost unheard of. The Old Catholic Church was founded during the 1870s in Germany as a result of the announcement of papal infallibility by the First Vatican Council in 1869-70 and took the name, 'The Union of Utrecht of Old Catholic Churches' and although it has no formal connection with the Holy See, it does maintain contact with and share many of the ideas of the Anglican Communion.

The beliefs of the Old Catholic Church differ from the much less liberal and conservative Church of Rome in its already mentioned views on homosexuality, the ordination of women priests, which it has done since 1996, and its refusal to condemn artificial contraception, preferring instead to leave it up to the individual couple. From this, it is not unreasonable to assume that Summers could more easily identify with the liberal attitude to homosexuality and, therefore, would feel better disposed to a church like this. However, he also became a member of a secret society called 'The Order of Chaeronea', which may give a clearer understanding of his motives in joining the Old Catholic Church and, of course, to the other charges laid against him. George Cecil Ives founded the Order of Chaeronea in 1897 with the intention of promoting homosexuality with a cultural and spiritual ethos, a concept which, at that time, was anathema to the general public.

Ives realised that there was little chance of the homosexual lifestyle being even close to acceptable in that era, so he decided to cultivate it secretly and, in this way, create an environment where homosexuals could mix and socialise with less fear of discovery and the consequent possibilities of ruin and probable imprisonment. To this end, he invented an elaborate set of rituals and initiations on similar lines to the Freemasons and other quasi-secret organisations that used signs and handshakes. Another thing that also strikes a resonant chord with Freemasonry was the development of a sign-word, in this case, 'AMRRHMO', which finds a close parallel with Masonic term, 'HTWSSSTKS', which is often found stamped on Masonic pennies. 'HTWSSSTKS', the original meaning of which supposedly lost, is remembered by the mnemonic, 'Hiram The Widows Son Sent Soon To King Solomon' or variants thereof. The meaning of the mnemonic, 'AMRRHMO', is unknown.

The keen interest that Summers apparently had in homosexuality and his possible paedophile inclinations aside, two of the things best known about him were his, at the time, unique translation of the odious Dominican witch-finding manual, the Malleus Malleficorum, and the publication of his best known work, The History of Witchcraft and Demonology (1926, reprinted in 1969). This was followed by a succession of works such as The Geography of Witchcraft (1927), A Popular History of Witchcraft (1937) and Witchcraft and Black Magic (1946). Summers was absolutely convinced that all witches, black or white, were irredeemably in league with Satan and his narrow definition of witchcraft provided no niceties of distinction between Wiccans, shamans, pagans and Satanists. As far as he was concerned, they were one and the same thing and thoroughly deserved everything coming to them and he was especially enthusiastic about the horrors of the Inquisition. Some, probably apocryphal, stories have hinted that he had a remit from a shadowy organisation within the Catholic hierarchy to seek out, expose and excoriate witchcraft at every opportunity, which, of course, he did, although this was almost certainly entirely of his own volition. Summers wrote that witches embodied every foul and perverse passion known to man, they were the epitome of evil, they were poisoners, worshipers of Satan, blasphemers, rapists, charlatans, bawds and abortionists.

He cultivated an air of mystery about himself and, in appearance, Summers was never less than striking and frequently walked around wearing a cloak with his long, silvery hair worn almost like a wig, while his fingers gleamed with his many jewelled rings. Oddly enough, he did not adopt clerical garb all that often and when he did, it was purely for effect. In spite of his short stature, he generated considerable charisma and people who met him were frequently in awe, something that he used to his advantage. The former wartime member of the British intelligence service and author of many novels on black magick, Dennis Wheatley, said quite categorically that Summers "inspired him with fear". It has been suggested that Wheatley based the character, the enigmatic Canon Copley-Style, in his extremely influential and alarming work, The Devil Rides Out, on Summers. In addition to his self-appointed role as an implacable foe of witchcraft and other evil doings, Summers also developed an interest in vampires and werewolves and espoused an unshakable belief in both of these legendary creatures, producing three books devoted to them, The Vampire, His Kith and Kin (1928), The Vampire in Europe (1929) and The Werewolf (1933).

In the course of his occult researches, it was inevitable that Summers should come into contact with Aleister Crowley, which he did, and, against all expectations, both men developed a friendship and mutual respect, meeting regularly to discus and air their totally different viewpoints. On second glance, perhaps it is not so surprising after all, since both of them were equally capable of plumbing the depths of the pit in their studies, both were extremely knowledgably in their respective fields and both had strange sexual proclivities. In addition, it is a fair bet that both men had grossly inflated egos and these meetings would probably allow them to preen and demonstrate their knowledge. This same ego-driven vanity is also why both enjoyed and deliberately cultivated a high public profile. It should come as no surprise to learn that, at one time, the almost ubiquitous Aleister Crowley attempted to set up his own religion using the title of 'Crowleyanity'.

Right until he died in August, 1948, the year after Crowley, Summers continued his vehement denunciation of magick and witchcraft while promoting the magickal beliefs of his church. He never faltered in his open admiration for the Inquisition and stoutly defended their record of brutality, murder and oppression. It was, after all, carried out with the best of intentions and sanctified in the name of God. There can be little doubt that had Summers been born a few centuries earlier, he would have equalled, and even surpassed, the efforts of De Guzman and Torquemada in his efforts to cleanse the planet from his narrow interpretation of sin. Thankfully, he was not. As a last, and possibly not too surprising, word about Summers, there were suggestions that, on December the 24th, 1918, he conducted a Black Mass assisted by two young men. This assertion, if true, shows the man as either a dedicated researcher, seeking to discover whether magick of this kind actually did produce results, or for the hypocritical pederast that he really was.

Chapter 19
British Witch Persecutions

Although the Inquisition in its European form never actually reached Britain, nevertheless, there were those who sought to winkle out unconventional ideas concerning belief about what was acceptable in terms of superstition in relation to religious orthodoxy. In Britain, this found expression when witchhunting fervour was actively encouraged following the introduction of a work entitled *Demonologie*, penned by the King James the IV of Scotland (James I of England) as a response to an incident that took place at North Berwick in Scotland. The king was convinced that witches had attempted to sink his ship by setting sail in a sieve when he travelled to Denmark (an example of sympathetic magick) and he also firmly believed that, since this failed to have the desired effect, magick would be worked against him by using toads' blood and other dubious charms and amulets.

The entire business came about through a confession forced from a girl, Gilly Duncan, who had practiced natural herbal healing techniques and fell foul of her superstitious employer who, in shades of the Inquisition, applied torture until she obligingly confessed to worshiping and receiving help from Satan. In her confession, she implicated a number of local women, including Agnes Sampson, Barbara Napier and Euphemia McLean. They, in turn, were rounded up and likewise tortured, some of it personally supervised by King James, until a final figure of seventy innocents stood accused of witchcraft and, worse still, supposedly conspiring against the king. Following a trial, they were all found guilty and sentenced to be executed by burning. The usual practice in Scotland (and elsewhere) was for the condemned to be strangled prior to the fire being started, but, as we have already seen, depending on who was facing execution, in many of these cases, they were not. The reason that the punishments were so severe was because King James was extremely superstitious and deathly afraid of the powers supposedly wielded by practitioners of magick like witches and warlocks. It was a mindset that mirrored opinions held in Europe.

What makes this especially troubling is that King James was a well-educated and intelligent man, every bit as intelligent as the hierarchy of the Church, but his capacity for superstitious belief was also extremely well developed. According to the Church, for their veneration of evil, witches were rewarded with various supposedly supernatural abilities, for example, the power to raise the dead, the ability to shape-shift into various animals, raise storms and cause sterility etc. Traditionally, witches met in covens of twelve members who were normally, but not exclusively, female. The number 12 is considered extremely significant in groups dedicated to magickal purposes. It should be made clear that the eagerness to punish witches and magicians was not only confined to the Catholic Church because the process was also eagerly embraced by the Protestant Church.

The reason for the significance of the number is probably due to the fact that 1 and 2 can be added to make 3, which is cognate with the Holy Trinity. This can be taken further when one considers that there are 12 months in the year, the day is 24 hours long (12+12), there are 12 houses in the Zodiac, there are 12 Sephiroth on the Cabbalistic Tree of Life, there are 12 tribes of Judah, Jesus was born at midnight (12am), Jesus preached in the temple aged 12, Jesus had 12 apostles, other Jesus prototypes mentioned in this book, i.e. Adonis, Osiris, Mithras etc., also had 12 disciples, there are 12 months in the year, King Arthur had 12 Knights of the Round Table.

The coven also had a leader, usually male, who would present himself as a horned creature, either a goat or stag. This was a clear indication of the nature worshipping origins of witchcraft, where Herne the Hunter and Pan (both traditional horned figures and fertility symbols and mentioned elsewhere) were invoked. Incidentally, the larger than life and semi-mythical figure of Robin Hood is based mainly on nature worship and his origins, once again, lead back to Osiris and, ultimately, Sun worship. The addition of the coven leader made the total to 13, which was also quite acceptable due to its association with bad fortune and less directly with Satan.

Incidentally, the popular image of witches travelling through the air on broomsticks has a rather less exotic explanation than might at first be thought. To induce a trance state, one of the many narcotic, plant-based preparations used by believers was the toxic, herbal narcotic, belladonna. Due to its inherent toxicity, this had to be applied internally, but, due to its poisonous nature, not orally, so, without going into too much detail, it was administered using the broom shaft. While it would be foolish to pretend that these and other practices did not happen, it is a fair bet that no matter at which level it was practiced, everyone was tarred with the same fearful brush. When the papal edict regarding witchcraft eventually arrived in Britain and was implemented, it lasted until the end of the 17th Century.

This era saw the appointment of a secular class of professional 'witchfinders'. The most notorious of these was Matthew Hopkins, a Puritan and the self-styled 'Witchfinder General'. Hopkins had trained as a lawyer, but, unfortunately, had seen better rewards in a different occupation. His hypocrisy, cruelty and brutality were legendary and, no doubt, the unfortunate victims of his zeal would have confessed to anything after he and his henchmen had finished with them. For all the ferocity of his campaign, it did not spread over a particularly large area, confining itself to the Midlands and Southeast of England, nor was it a lengthy affair. Surprisingly, Hopkins was only twenty-eight years old when he finally died, taking with him the worst excesses of this disgraceful period in British history.

As previously mentioned, although there was an element of devil worship involved, for the most part, the so-called witches throughout the Middle Ages were either old women with a talent for healing the sick, using herbal cures, or hermits and recluses. The mantle of 'witch' was also given to midwives, especially those who practiced with no formal training. If you bear in mind the era, the Middle Ages, this is hardly surprising, given the rituals, secrecy and superstition surrounding childbirth at that time. It is also another sad reflection on the Catholic Church that it strongly disapproved of, to the point of specifically forbidding, any form of pain relief being administered to women in labour. They decided it was a woman's duty to suffer as Eve had suffered. Even although it emerged in medieval times, this belief lasted for a remarkably long time in Church dogma and further serves to highlight the misogyny that was rampant in the Catholic hierarchy. The ambivalent attitude of the Church to females is directly responsible for Mary Magdalene being portrayed as a prostitute and woman of easy virtue.

On the subject of the Magdalene, although the Church knows perfectly well that she was not a whore and will admit so if pushed, this utterly incorrect and unjustified impression still survives to this day.

The confusion, paranoia and fear that were rampant during this early period led to many totally blameless people being branded as witches. This could be for almost any reason, from people falling ill to farm animals becoming lame. If these happenings had no obvious cause, then the blame, quite obviously, had to lie with a supernatural agency, namely a witch. Since the perpetrator had to be found, this led to finger pointing and a culprit, usually old and female, was blamed. The methods of extracting a confession were uniformly agonising and humiliating. The most frequently employed method was 'pricking', which involved jabbing the unfortunate victim with a thin metal skewer. This was because a witch was said to have a mark made by the devil somewhere on their body. The mark was supposed to be impervious to pain and 'pricking' was a sure way to find it. This practice would obviously leave the victim running with blood, which, to the inquisitors, was neither here nor there and did not count as part of the torture anyway.

One example of the profound malice of the witchfinders concerns one unfortunate woman who had been accused of witchcraft, but on whom no obvious blemishes could be detected. Undeterred, the witchfinder decided that the woman 'looked like a witch' (whatever that means) and proceeded to torture her anyway until a confession was forthcoming. In this era, it was a distinct disadvantage to possess red hair, which was a sure sign that the person having this hair colour, especially if they were female, was probably involved in unsavoury practices of some kind anyway. This was based on the ancient myth that redheads obtained their colouring through basking in the flames of Hell fire.

The fact that they were almost certainly freckled as well meant that the witchfinder and his cohorts were spoiled for choice when looking for a suitable mark. Similar accusations of witchcraft have occasionally been made about Mary Magdalene, who is traditionally depicted with a luxurious mane of red hair. Those who speak in defence of the Magdalene say that her colouring was more likely to be dark or swarthy, since she was of Semitic stock. While true, this ignores the fact that the gene responsible for producing red hair is found all over the world and I have seen red-headed Arabs. Similarly the genetic defect that produces albinos is not peculiar only to certain ethnic groups. Unfortunately, those afflicted with this condition in some parts of Africa are in fear of their lives because traditional magick regards their body parts as possessing great magickal power and pay handsomely to have them murdered to obtain the necessary parts.

Other forms of 'proof' of involvement in witchcraft included the presence of an extra nipple, where the witch would suckle her 'familiar' or demonic assistant, normally a cat or a toad. Perhaps the worst form of discovering the innocence or guilt of a witch was the 'dipping test', which involved binding the accused and either throwing them into a river or attaching them to a length of wood and submerging them in water. They reasoned that if the accused was innocent then she would sink, but if she were to float, the water, being pure, would reject this embodiment of evil and refuse to accept it.

In these more enlightened times, it is difficult to believe that people could be so wilfully stupid and gullible, but in those dark days, there was little education and much fear created by the brimstone and hellfire sermons dispensed by the ranting zealots styling themselves as witchfinders. In reality, it would not have been difficult to obtain a fervent following among the populace, since to show no great interest and enthusiasm (let alone contempt) for the unbalanced ranting was a sure way to invite a personal visit from the local witchfinder.

All through this horrific era, the religious authorities sat back and looked on with tacit, and sometimes not so tacit, approval. Its dirty work was done and it did not soil its hands. It may seem odd, but the tactics employed by witchfinders seem to have much in common with those of the demon-banishing Evangelical and Pentecostal preachers discussed earlier in the book, but at least the outcome is different.

Witchcraft still flourishes in various guises, ranging from the Wiccan or white witch, indulging in a spiritual, gentle and natural way of life, to the opposite end of the spectrum, where, as before, witchcraft and Satanism walk the same, dangerous path. It is understandable why people are attracted to this darker, dangerous, more malignant side. For the vast majority, it can only be a need for money, power or sex and the adrenaline rush of the unknown and, perhaps, a combination of all four.

It is easy to imagine the novice undergoing his or her initiation into the workings of the coven, standing in darkness in the circle, blindfold, dry-mouthed, tingling with anticipation and fear, the scent of incense heavy in the air. The half-remembered whispered instructions, oaths to be taken and contracts signed and all, ultimately, for power and secrets that might give them control over their fellow human beings. It is, in many ways, similar to a physical addiction, when the initial thrill has worn off, when the plateau is reached and the need for a bigger 'hit' becomes a necessity.

When this happens, the need to delve deeper and deeper into occult practices increases until a point of no return is reached and the initiate must eventually decide whether to stop or take the final step and perhaps become involved in the ritual sacrifice of a human being. There is no doubt that this can and does happen. It is presumed that a least some of those who go missing each year, never to be found, are ritually slaughtered on the altars of Satanic groups. Fortunately, although this type of coven is real enough, they are the exception rather than the rule, but most cities and large towns will probably have a coven of one sort or another. Most of them are little more than an excuse for dressing up, drinking and wife swapping, but the remainder will be more serious and dedicated and include everything from the white witches, who are, at least, well intentioned, to those grimmer gatherings whose purpose is quite the opposite.

Chapter 20
The Persistence of Magickal Beliefs

Sharing a faint resonance with an earlier chapter, where the subject of sacred items used as part of a religious/magickal process was mentioned in a modern context, we also find the use of traditional, sacred artefacts used as magickal charms. Although these practices are no longer quite as prominent as they were, they never entirely disappeared, especially use of holy relics to invoke cures etc. and, in spite of the best efforts of the clergy, neither has the influence of Wicca and witchcraft, although it is fairly easy to see why alchemy, in its original form, faded into oblivion. As conventional science progressed, largely, if inadvertently, assisted by the early experimental dabbling of these scientist-priests and philosophers, the increasing difficulty of their quest became obvious. To be sure, although nowadays we, with superior modern technology, produce results and materials that these men could only dream about, despite specious claims to the contrary, we still cannot produce gold from base metals. In retrospect, though, to find the Church actively involved with what it itself deemed as major heresy is no real surprise.

However, it is blatantly obvious that the origins of modern pharmacology, metallurgy and chemistry have their roots in witchcraft, shamanism and alchemy and the majority of medieval scientists and doctors were also regarded as borderline magicians and alchemists. As far as European alchemists are concerned, there were many, but the previously mentioned churchman, Roger Bacon, notwithstanding, there were characters like the near legendary Dr John Dee, Phillippus Aureolus Theophrastus Bombastus von Hohenheim (better known as Paracelsus) and who, due to his overbearing arrogance, may have lent his name to the term 'bombastic', although there are other suggested derivations for this.

Incidentally, in a further example of his self-regard, the nickname, Paracelsus, means equal or greater than Celsus, who was a Roman physician from the First Century known for his medical tracts. There was also Heinrich Kunrath, an individual of great piety who admired Dr Dee for his supposed contact with angels and even such luminaries and founders of the Royal Society as Isaac Newton and Elias Ashmole, who were also involved in the search for the elusive Philosophers' Stone. All of these men were polymaths and all of them left their indelible mark on the history of science in all its diversity.

Another link that connected these individuals was their certainty that the whole of creation was based on number, proportion and even music, heretical concepts in their era that find considerably greater relevance today. Indeed, in the time of these pioneers the relatively innocuous science of mathematics still carried the taint of magick about it and was viewed with great suspicion by the ever-inflexible Church. The alchemists were well aware of the concepts devised by the Greek mathematician and astronomer, Pythagoras, whose philosophy suggested that number and ratio were above all else in the cosmos and even linked into how music and musical intervals obeyed mathematical rules, in this case the ratio of 3:2 or 'Pythagorean tuning'. This concept gave rise to such quotations as, 'The Music of The Spheres', something that was later reinforced by Johannes Keppler (1571-1630) when he made the connection between sacred geometry, astronomy and harmonics which he called 'Harmonice Mundi' or 'the harmony of the world'.

John Dee carried this further when he observed that, "The entire universe is like a lyre tuned by some excellent artificer." Isaac Newton thought that the universe was "a cryptogram set by the almighty" and, in much more recent times, the great scientific communicator and quantum physicist, Professor Michio Kaku, wisely commented that, "The universe is like a cathedral resonating to the sound of superstrings." Resonance and frequency - is that the secret of the alchemical process, is it really as simple as that, is that what they sought but never found? Even the semi-legendary electrical genius, Nikola Tesla, commented, when one of his students asked if there was one fundamental truth, that the only real secrets of the universe were "vibration, resonance and frequency".

The scale of these ratios goes from the immense to the subatomic, however the truth of the matter might even go back right to the beginning of time itself. The Bible says that, 'In the beginning was the word, and the word was with God and the word was God'. As I said at the outset, I have drawn religion into this debate through necessity and to give context, even although it really has no place here, but this particular biblical quotation does give cause for consideration and reflection, more for what it does not say rather than for what it does and this may well have been deliberate. Might it actually reveal that this ancient document that was written by man is actually carrying a kind of 'ancient code' hidden among and interlaced with what is written in its pages? Might it even have been expressly set out to convey this truth for those with the eyes to see?

According to the Bible, 'In the beginning was the word' infers that the word made a sound, so it might be more accurate to say, 'In the beginning was the sound of the word'. If that is indeed the case, then the concept of music and sound being an intrinsic part of reality is unquestionable. One only has to consider just how effectively music can be used as a tool when it affects our emotions to induce fear, anger, peace and love and, depending on the intensity and frequency used, it can also kill. If the universe (uni-verse, meaning literally 'one word', even the name of it is redolent with clues as to its origins) is constructed according to measurable harmonic principles, then it becomes reasonable to ask who constructed it? This, of course, nods toward the use of spells and incantations in magick, especially where rhythmic chanting is used. One of the words used to infer the use of a spell is to 'en-chant'. Is this yet another clear hint of what is involved?

The components that comprise human beings are also constructed according to individual frequencies. Therefore we are, in a sense, attuned to the reality that we inhabit. Might this mean that to unlock the secrets of magick and even alchemy, what we must do is learn to manipulate these frequencies of the numbers involved to achieve mastery over them? The ultimate ubiquity of number even stretches to the use of language, the very thing that permits communication. When Gematria, the ancient science of numerical divination, is applied to language, one finds that phrases and words having the same or similar meanings possess identical numerical values. Why should this be? To use current phraseology, this is 'the elephant in the room', the enigma that looms so large in front of us so that we cannot see it. What is even more astonishing is that these early seekers after truth could sense this almost by instinct alone, while the powers that governed them sought to stifle the self-evident under a veil of superstitious fear and ruthless oppression.

The truth is that Pythagoras and those like him understood that the mystical nature of numbers developed from the aeons-old and instinctive tradition that understanding numbers gave humanity a degree of control over, and understanding of, the world and even the cosmos around it. He did not suddenly have a blinding 'eureka moment' of revelation, but he did develop, expand and improve upon the much earlier efforts of our ancestors in ancient India, Egypt and even prehistoric Europe. With our privilege of hindsight, we can appreciate that the use of numbers was considered magickal even before Pythagoras popularised and refined it into a semblance of science. It developed slowly and in purely practical guises, e.g. the number of geographical features to pass before changing direction, the number of stars in a constellation, the so-called 'megalithic yard' and the dimensions used by stonemasons etc.

A building constructed by rule of thumb alone would never equal the beauty and symmetry of one that had been constructed to exact measurements. Small wonder, then, that the masons were so keen to conceal their 'magickal' secrets, especially those that made use of the 'Golden Mean' and other sacred ratios. In terms of sheer survival, the use of numbers was vital in understanding the seasons. Without appreciating the importance of numbers, those who worked the land could not know the time to successfully plant seeds and then harvest them. The seasons did serve a purpose, but their time scale was too wide and imprecise. It was the understanding of numbers that finally marked humanity out from the animals as the rulers of the planet. Hopefully, the same understanding of numbers and equations will not also be humanity's death knell.

Chapter 21
Magick and Church Ritual

One of the main sticking points in aligning religion and magick is the impression that the rituals used during a church service and what happens in a ceremony involving magick are quite separate and this is not necessarily the case. There are many striking similarities. In essence, the priest, rabbi or imam acts as a focus directing the prayers of his flock to invoke some kind of response from an invisible entity. Sometimes it is purely to praise and glorify their version of God and sometimes it is designed to ask for some kind of intercession designed to cause something to happen. This can be for any purpose, for instance, for an individual who is suffering, for the benefit of a group, to stop a war, to comfort the dying, to end a drought, literally anything is permissible providing it is intended for good.

However, it is certain that this powerful invocation technique has also been used for evil as well, especially in times long gone when the power of God was sought to, for example, encourage the wholesale murder of heretics or anyone else disagreeing with official Church teachings. In very recent times, there is one example in particular where biblical references were made in relation to equipment used by the US and British armed forces. This refers to sniper sights designated as 'ACOG' (Advanced Combat Optical Gunsight) manufactured by the American company, Trijicon. This arms company saw fit to include two such references on the equipment they produce, one to John 8:12 and also to 2 Corinthians 4:6. Both of these references, which refer to spiritual illumination, are part of the respective stock numbers for two different types of gunsight and are encoded as **JN8:12** and **2COR4:6**. The company involved was quite open about the practice, because the idea had been implemented by the owner, who held deeply conservative religious views and considered the references as a form of additional aid and protection for the troops, which, as far as it went, was well intentioned.

The governments of the US and the UK have asked for these references to be removed from any further items they purchase. From an alternative viewpoint, the act of including them can easily be interpreted as an invocation to a supernatural agency (in this case, the Christian God) to assist the troops who use these items - in other words, a spell. In the case of these two gunsights, they are used in Afghanistan and Iraq and are potentially an unimaginable propaganda gift to the fundamentalist Islamists who form the hard core of Taleban and Al-Qaeda fighters in these countries. Both of these groups have insisted from the outset (incorrectly) that the conflicts in these unfortunate nations are an extension of the ancient Christian religious Crusades and the inclusion of these references only serves to help corroborate their claims.

Before leaving this rather contentious point, it is as well to consider that the zealots comprising the forces of extreme Islam also bedeck themselves with protection by using quotes from the Qur'an, usually in the form of green headbands with the quotes in white Arabic script. During the Second World War, the majority of the world's armed forces were issued with a Bible as part of their kit, presumably to bring comfort to those that had faith, although it could be interpreted as using it to legitimise war. Irrespective of who uses it, there is no essential difference between this methodology and the invocations conducted during a magickal ceremony, when the leader of the group draws power from their congregation/coven and offers this to any deity considered appropriate.

In general, these groups use a variation on nature magick to work their intentions, which are normally for the benefit of the group or, like the Church, for a beneficial purpose. We also find this in conjunction with Chaos Magick, where the essence of the wish is written in the form of a 'sigil'. Briefly, a sigil is a drawn or written symbol based on the letters comprising the words of a spell. The words of the spell/wish/desire are gradually reduced in number by removing repeating letters and sometimes even some of the words. The remainder is then formed into either a symbol or a single word. This 'condensate' or 'residue' of the original incantation is then considered to contain the potency and intent of the entire sentence. We will return to the subject of Chaos Magick a little later, but in much greater detail.

The best analogy would be to consider the culinary practice of making 'reductions' in the process of cooking a dish. This reduces the liquor from the ingredients in the original recipe into a highly-flavoured concentrate. It is precisely the same concept, although the outcome is obviously different. It also makes one wonder if the same comparisons could be made with prayers, because it is logical to assume that the same procedure would produce the same results. However, what is done with the finished product is solely attributable to whoever is using it. This surely is yet another example of the striking similarities between clergymen and magicians. Interestingly, the concept of condensates and residues resonates powerfully with the chemical processes required in the production of the Philosophers' Stone, which is one of the main functions of alchemy and could be argued is a kind of esoteric cookery.

Another factor to consider is that the sigil, whether made from a prayer or a spell, is indifferent to its end use. Like all magick, it consists of potential and nothing more, as with everything else relating to this subject, it is the purpose to which it is put that defines its nature. Incidentally, apparently none of this has anything whatsoever to do with Satanism, which, although based on similar lines, has an entirely different, usually hedonistic, ethos. Even here, we find the occasional Satanist who will refute claims that their system of belief has anything to do with the 'Black Mass'. This philosophy was promoted by, among others, such self-styled magicians as the already mentioned Anton Szandor le Vey, founder of the 'Church of Satan'.

Paganism and the Church

There is as additional factor found in many Christian churches that, by rights, should have no place there, but may shine an unintended source of light upon the origins of the Christian faith. In churches, especially the older ones that were built while echoes of the 'Old Ways' still had some relevance, there are representations of a pagan figure called 'The Green Man'. This curious figure, which also occurs in Wiccan belief, can often be seen as a carved bas-relief face, dotted around church buildings and usually intertwined with leaves and other kinds of foliage. It is very prominently displayed in the structure of the previously mentioned Rosslyn Chapel. In fact, if one knows where to look, there is a set of these images that progresses round the inside walls of the chapel in a clockwise or 'deasil' (sometimes expressed as deosign) manner. The faces depict the aging process from young to old, which both signifies the rising and setting sun and, interpreted symbolically, can also be interpreted as the dying and rising God - in other words the cycle of renewal.

There is no dispute regarding why it is incorporated into the fabric of churches. It is a fertility symbol carried over from the nature (and sun) worshiping origins of the Christian faith that were eventually subsumed into its developing canon of belief. It is also relevant to the thanksgiving services that are still common in many churches in the late summer to celebrate the harvest and, as we have seen, have very obvious magickal roots. Another element associated with the pagan roots of religion is seen, especially in England, in the late summer around harvest time, when groups of men dress up in traditional costume and, accompanied by the 'Hobby Hoss', another symbol of fertility, dance, sing and caper thought the street of many rural villages. Unfortunately, in most cases, those involved in these ceremonies do not fully understand the symbolic nature of what they do. To them, it is a custom carried out purely for its own sake with no idea of its profound, magickal underpinnings.

The same is true of dances round the May Pole where the fertility based origins of the custom are hidden away behind a sanitised version of the truth, and it has to be said that it is perhaps best that it is this way. The original maypole, with the gaily-coloured streamers floating from the top was, of course, a graphic representation of the penis ejecting sperm. The purpose of the maids dancing around this phallic symbol is obvious, however, the ancient outcome of what was being celebrated traditionally came to a head when those participating in the ceremony, the young men and women, gradually stole away in their pairs to the forest to consummate the closing of the day. Nine months later, their belated contribution to the harvest duly appeared.

Chapter 22
The Gnostics

The main source of background knowledge relating to gnostic practices originally came from the early fathers of the fledgling Christian Church, like Bishop Clement of Alexandria, who was also an early follower of Gnostic Christianity. These early sages, or perhaps censors might be a better term, had, through self interest, every reason to downplay its relevance, so, after the Nag Hammadi codices (or texts) were found in 1945, the information contained in them cast a very different light on gnostic beliefs. What was in the texts may have encouraged the emergence of a variety of New Age and quasi-magickal movements, including esoteric Christianity. Before launching into this, admittedly brief, explanation, the reader should be aware that what will be revealed makes it obvious that we are entering an unfamiliar cosmology inhabited by strange and unfamiliar entities.

Despite the obvious similarities, there is no doubt that the authorities who administer the various schisms of monotheistic belief categorically deny (or refuse to concede) that there is anything magickal about what they do. The truth is that they cannot and dare not even consider the comparison, despite the fact that all the variations of their God lie in one single entity. This is also found when one looks at the roots of gnostic belief, which is, more often than not, also associated with magick or, if not magick, then mysticism, which, in some circumstances, is the same thing. Although not an easily accessible subject, the concept of gnosticism lies behind many of the strands of mystical belief that have developed around, and almost certainly preceded, all strands of religious faith, but, specifically, the monotheistic strains. The fundamental truth behind this type of belief is that there is indeed a God or, at least, some kind of central, unifying and controlling power at the very heart of the cosmos and we can make contact with it.

The problems start to surface in the manner in which this is achieved. Gnostics believe, quite logically, that there is no reason why they should not achieve spiritual union (gnosis) with the supreme spirit on a personal, one to one basis; in other words discover their own personal Jesus/saviour/supreme being. In the case of the theology used by the Catholic Church, since Jesus is part of the Holy Trinity of Father, Son and Holy Spirit, then this means that identifying with Christ automatically means achieving a personal union with God. This, in turn, implies that there is no need for mediation, whether it be through priests, cardinals, popes or rituals or any other part of Church apparatus, therefore, it is regarded as a major heresy. It is something that would apply to any belief system, whether it is Christian, Jewish, Islamic, monotheistic or pantheistic.

The reason that it is regarded as a heresy is usually because the person so engaged is endangering their soul or some other spiritual hazard. The truth is rather more mundane; it is about control, plain and simple, and is absolutely typical of organisations with much to lose, but a great deal to gain (or maintain). Once people start to see beyond dogma and experience with their own set of truths, then they are freed from the yoke of joyless guilt and fear that many religions foist on their members in the name of their doctrines. This is by no means confined to Roman Catholicism and is found in many Christian fundamentalist and Bible-literalist organisations that seem to take a perverse pride in interpreting scripture in as depressing and austere a manner as possible then enacting it in their daily lives. Once again, this perverse and unnecessary take on theology is found in most of the other faiths.

Might it be stretching the point too far to observe that, even here, the strains of the familiar gnostic 'as above so below' mantra are heard, only in this case, the 'as above so below' comes from the word of God (as they see it) who, of course, lives on high. This view tends to sideline the millennia-long series of attempts by our ancient ancestors to 'draw down' the heavens and attempt to recreate them here on Earth. This is why archaeologists continue to discover and sometimes reinterpret stone circles and vast monuments arranged to mirror the alignment of the stars and the solar system. It is also noted that the heart of our planetary system, the Sun, has spawned innumerable religions and cults since the dawn of time and is still honoured and recognised, albeit unconsciously, in the haloes depicted above the heads of the Holy Family, the saints and even in the crowns still worn by royal houses. It is further evidence, should it be needed, that these ancient beliefs and customs have become encoded and hard-wired into our race memories.

The branches of gnostic belief that often spring to mind when the subject is broached, although there are many, are the Manicheans, the Johannites, the Bogomils and the Cathars, all of which were similar in outlook. As far as they were concerned, the only true God was purely spiritual, with no possible physical connections. This meant that the world in which they lived was the product of another God, the Rex Mundi or 'God of the World', which equates with Satan and was, therefore, imperfect and flawed. This interpretation included themselves and every aspect of their physical lives and this was one of the main areas on which the Church concentrated. In general, though, those who chose the gnostic path avoided sex because it was a physical act of gratification and not always associated purely with the need to procreate. They were also vegetarian, because anything that came from animals was the product of copulation. It has been argued that, because of their rejection of sex, if left to their own devices, their beliefs would have died out of their own accord anyway, through an eventual lack of members.

They were also, by inclination, ascetic and avoided anything that might give pleasure, which, once again, was seen as a physical failing. Their Christian critics (mainly monks and other ecclesiastics) were on shaky ground in this particular aspect of their attack, because they did exactly the same thing and for much the same reasons, so there had to be a clear divide. This was resolved by the Christian ascetics announcing that the gnostics were (A) incorrectly interpreting scripture or (B) were simply liars who participated in secret orgies. This was a risky strategy on the part of the Christians, who might well have been piqued by the prurient interests and base pleasures of the lay population, but, as we shall see, in telling how gnostic beliefs developed, there are clear similarities with what was to follow.

Although, like the various faiths that came after them, there were slight differences in outlook, mainly in the severity in which they applied their beliefs, the outline went something like this: the 'Pure God' created spiritual beings called 'aeons', who populated heaven. This continued quite happily for a time, but eventually things went wrong and, evidently, even though created in a state of spiritual perfection, there were some bad seeds and the youngest aeon, called Sophia (the name equates to 'wisdom' in some schools of thought), got pregnant and gave birth to Yaldaboath, sometimes called 'The Demiurge', a kind of arrogant and imperfect aeon/artisan, who had a foot in both the spiritual and the physical realms. According to 'The Hypostasis of the Archons' or 'The Reality of the Rulers', from the Nag Hammadi Library, Codex II, translated by the American academic, Bentley Layton, "The Demiurge is blind; because of his power, ignorance and arrogance. It is I who am God; there is none apart from me." When he said this, he sinned against the entirety. And this speech got up to the Incorruptibility (a higher form of being, in effect, the 'Pure God' of dualistic belief) then there was a voice that came forth from the Incorruptibility, saying, "You are mistaken, Samael" which is "god of the blind".

This observation, while not exactly crystal clear, appears to infer that, although the Demiurge was still supernatural, he was subservient a higher authority, viz. the Pure God. It is thought that the concept of the Demiurge is attributable to the legendary Greek philosopher, Plato, some of whose musings are found at the core of all gnostic traditions, although, admittedly, sometimes paraphrased. From this, it becomes clear that deep consideration regarding the manner in which the universe began is not solely the product of modern thinking and typifies the inbuilt necessity of human beings to ask profound questions regarding our place in it. The only difference is that we, with our current scientific knowledge and equipment, can see infinitely further and, to a large extent, verify what we see. Prior to the birth of the Demiurge, there was no universe, so, in a sense, one could say that this being was responsible for the Big Bang, the creation of the universe and all it contains. This implies that, if the Demiurge created the physical universe, he/she/it/they must therefore be the Rex Mundi or the 'God of the World' rejected by the Cathars, etc.

This, of course, is (or was) completely at odds with conventional, religious thinking and is, therefore, another reason that such teachings are heretical. Unfortunately, although the mainstream has largely accepted the evidence of science as irrefutable, there are still hard-line Bible literalists and Creationists who cling desperately to their views, despite a mountain of overwhelming evidence to the contrary. As far as the Big Bang is concerned, despite being a tacitly approved Church version of Creation, it brings the reality of this supreme Creator God (CG), existing quite separately outside time and space, into sharp focus and also raises some interesting questions. Did the hypothetical CG bring about the unimaginable cataclysm of the Big Bang as an interested bystander, the director of a gargantuan scientific experiment, if you like, or is the CG the singularity at the very core of the Big Bang? Or, if the 'interested bystander' was the Pure God of spirit alone, then why was the inferior Demiurge allowed to create the universe? Or did the Pure God permit it simply because it could not stop it? The possibilities and permutations are endless and enigmatic.

The main part of the gnostic process is, of course, achieving unity with the essence of the divine and, in so doing, becoming part of creation itself. Once again, we should be aware that this is not new (in spiritual terms, very little is) and was the purpose behind many Eastern belief systems that also set out to achieve a state of union with the cosmos, all of which long predated the emergence of Christianity or its predecessor, Judaism. The saying that developed from Eastern philosophy became 'All is One' and, indeed, it is and once communion has been achieved, the sensation is one of immense knowledge, peace and tranquillity.

The Demiurge also had assistance from beings called the 'archons' and created the human race, in Greek the word, 'archon', means literally 'one of the nine chief magistrates', sometimes translated as 'petty rulers'. The race created by these beings was alive in a physical sense, but asleep spiritually. However, inside each and every one was a tiny ember of the original state of spiritual grace, which could still be re-ignited into seeking salvation. It seems that the concept of an original, single source that links all of us is common to most, if not all, belief systems. One has to ask, which came first here, the chicken or the egg? What is described appears to be an alternative account of how Lucifer and his fallen angels were cast out of Heaven, the Nephilim and how they interbred with human beings, the temptation of the Adam and Eve and original sin. Although not completely interchangeable, there are very clear similarities between the two accounts, however, both still support the theory that the human race did not evolve through natural selection, but may well have been the product of some external interference. Although that is one interpretation of the facts as set out in the Book of Genesis, the accepted religious view is that, rather than evolve naturally, we, as a race, along with the universe, simply sprang into being at the command of God.

At this point, we should perhaps pause to reflect on one of the Nag Hammadi codices, which were a spectacular revelation in every sense, because, as with the Dead Sea Scrolls, their implications cast profound doubts over what has become accepted as spiritual, religious and magickal truth. The texts were discovered by accident in 1945 near the town of Nag Hammadi in Upper Egypt by two youngsters, who were looking for fertiliser near some caves. Their find was contained in a large, sealed, clay vessel and comprised twelve leather-bound collections of papyrus parchments, divided into fifty-two separate treatises, mainly dealing with gnostic subjects. Originally, the youths did not report their find and intended to sell the documents as a money-making enterprise, but there are reports that their mother burned some of the find in case there was some kind of curse associated with them, a fate that befell a few of the Dead Sea Scrolls, although for slightly different reasons. Although there are fifty-two of these parchments, those that have become best known are, The Gospel of Philip, The Gospel of Thomas, The Gospel of Truth and the aforementioned The Hypostasis of the Archons.

Chapter 23
The Cornerstone of all Magick

As with the various doctrines that support almost all types of belief, history implies that there are usually common traits that link them, although this is an idea that might be resisted. First, we should perhaps look at Chaos Magick and how it came to exist. Accepted wisdom says that the concept of Chaos Magick developed in the 1970s in West Yorkshire, in England, following a meeting between Peter Carroll and Ray Sherwin. These two men went on to create an organisation called 'The Illuminates of Thanateros' (IOT), devoted to the development and promotion of their beliefs. This is well and good, but the founding spirit of Chaos Magick actually came from the practices of the mystic and artist, Austin Osman Spare, who had developed a system of magick involving sigils, the function of which we have already looked at, and gnostic trances. The timing of its appearance is fortunate, since it occurred on the leading edge of the cultural explosion that occurred during the 1960s and '70s and brought with it a greatly enhanced acceptance of many spiritual ideas and philosophies.

Unfortunately, Spare died before his work was fully recognised, although the techniques he developed served to encourage other aspiring magicians to elaborate and expand on his methods. Some practitioners of this magickal system consider that there is nothing 'supernatural' in what they do and that when changes occur in accordance with their desires, then the effect has been induced through natural forces. This stance has, unsurprisingly, produced some marked differences of opinion within the ranks of practicing magicians, and it is easy to see why, but this depends very much on how one interprets the word, 'supernatural'. It may be that using the definition applied by Chaos Magicians is an attempt to demystify the process and remove the implications attached to religion and superstition. It may even be an attempt to reclassify it as a branch of technology, which is an idea that may actually hold some promise. Nevertheless, its successful operation does involve areas that have, as yet, no direct parallels in the scientific world, although that may change.

As we have seen, the person desiring profound, personal, spiritual knowledge (gnosis) must first enter a state where this is possible and it is exactly the same for practitioners of Chaos Magick. Both must achieve an altered state of awareness and this can be achieved in two main ways, comprising 'Inhibitory Gnosis' and 'Exitory Gnosis', but there is another and less well-known method called 'Indifferent Vacuity'. Although the first two methods involve altering consciousness and awareness, 'Inhibitory Gnosis' requires the use of yoga-based breathing techniques allied with relaxation and self-hypnosis and can also involve the use of deliberate sleep deprivation. Lack of sleep automatically raises the levels of neurotransmitters, like serotonin, which, in itself, may be responsible for the visions etc. It may also contribute to sightings of ghosts and ETs, both of which are frequently seen either at night or when someone is tired. Fasting can also be used plus the careful use of hallucinogens. The second method, 'Exitory Gnosis', is a deliberate attempt to overload the senses through a constant bombardment of powerful emotions induced by repetitive chanting and drumming. The use of hyperventilation and chemical enhancement can also be added to achieve the desired effect. Many of the techniques mentioned in the first two methods, apart from the deliberate use of chemicals, will, once again, force the brain to react by producing various chemicals in order to protect itself.

The third method, 'Indifferent Vacuity', is a strange hybrid that involves the practitioner entering the gnostic trance state (the means are not all that important, although some practitioners will swear by their own tried and tested methods), then try to remain on the outside while 'harvesting' what occurs inside the gnostic state/trance/spell. This rather bizarre technique, which cannot be easy, is like splitting your consciousness in two then using one part to monitor the other and it is thought to afford the seeker a measure of protection should things go wrong. The use of hallucinogens, even in the form of incense and essential oils, etc., although effective, are frowned upon by purists as 'unnatural', because other 'natural' methods can be used to attain the same trance state, although this can take considerably longer. The natural techniques are supposedly more satisfying and intimate because those who use them regard the process as nature communing with nature, perhaps inducing the body to reconnect with the whole, but hallucinogens are certainly much quicker.

As an adjunct to this fascinating crossover of magickal and religious practices and as a slight, but still relevant, diversion, it may also be legitimate to mention that the Catholic Church uses pleasant smelling incense during rituals associated with the Mass. The main one is the already discussed ritual associated with transubstantiation; the incense contains such fragrant substances as myrrh, frankincense and resins like copal. Frankincense is associated with the Sun and also the male principle, while myrrh is associated with healing and the female principle. These attributions exactly define many ancient mystical and magickal traditions attached to the two sexes: man is the Sun, while woman is the caring and nurturing healer. Copal, on the other hand, is a generic title for a variety of granular resins that occur in a range of colours and are used for purification and cleansing the spirit and also items used in the ceremonies. The smoke from the incense is ostensibly used as a visual sign that the prayers of the faithful are being carried up to Heaven. Of course, its more important use, and the one not quite so well acknowledged, involves cleansing the area of evil spirits and other undesirable elements. The ritual use of incense, which long predates its Christian function, seems to stem from the ceremonies of the ancient Egyptians and it was also widely used in China and throughout Southeast Asia.

We also find that overtly magickal practices also use incenses for a number of reasons, some positive and other less so. Satanic groups use various substances, but mainly 'patchouli', also and perhaps significantly called 'graveyard dust', to invoke a variety of demons for use in clairvoyance, healing and, if necessary, to throw a curse. Once again, the use of incense is intended to signify that something remarkable or special is about to take place, a time when 'change' can occur. Incense is also utilised in pagan and Wiccan settings, where it is employed for similar, but less threatening, purposes and the 'energy' contained in the fragrance of the incense can be used to enhance the magick being performed. The Wiccan interpretation of incense usage comes from the assumption that the material comprising the incense combines the four earthly elements of fire (to burn it), water (produced while it burns), air (which carries the fragrance) and earth (where its constituents grow), so it fits snugly into their magickal philosophy.

Another frequently ignored aspect of incense is its use as a hallucinogen or as a carrier for hallucinogenic substances, whose frequently distinctive smells are masked by the fragrance of other additives. Plants like salvia and cannabis were, and still are, used in this context, although the use of cannabis would not ordinarily be employed in public places, in case the authorities decided to intervene, but so-called 'legal highs', like salvia are still used because it is legal and readily obtainable. The reasons for this are not difficult to appreciate, because if the intention is to produce altered states of consciousness, then this is one method other than actually consuming some hallucinogenic potion that is effective while still allowing its other, less obvious, properties and attributes to be used.

Incidentally, it may not always be the purely hallucinogenic effects that produce the desired effect, because some of the plants used in making incense also release pheromones, whose purpose, if combined with hallucinogens, may well produce some fascinating and magickal possibilities. The range of plants used in incense making (and the equally and sometimes more effective essential oils) include aloe, rosemary, mugwart, laurel, the previously mentioned salvia, cloves, cinnamon, cedar, ambergris, balsam, rockrose, storax and many more. Of these substances, the last four, ambergris, balsam, rockrose and storax, all contain chemicals called 'pheromone analogues', which may account for their unusual properties. It may be of interest to learn that vanilla, a commonly use and pleasant flavouring, also has attractant properties if appropriately prepared and used. A list of incense related natural compounds is included at the end of the book.

It is also true to say that the concept of Chaos Magick is almost anarchic, mechanistic, 'post-punk' and even in accord with the chaos theory of quantum physics in its ethos. This is in total and absolute contrast with the ceremonial and structured 'high magick' practiced by the aforementioned Ordo Templi Orientis (OTO) and the Hermetic Order of the Golden Dawn, which, as we have seen, are more aligned to the rituals and degrees used in Freemasonry. The stripped down, back to basic approach of the Chaos Magicians is arguably closer to the intent of the original shamans and animists who attempted to influence their surroundings by direct contact. It is a paradigm that creates a clear difference between them and the elaborate and perhaps over-hyped ceremonies associated with the OTO and the Golden Dawn and this is often reflected in the way in which they interact with, and are perceived by, the world.

For example, it is likely that a Chaos Magician would be more interested in 'heavy metal' music and denim than the gentler folk-inspired music favoured by, say, Wiccans. The traditional and rather old-fashioned magickal values upheld by the OTO and Golden Dawn tends to suggest that they might favour classical music and other more conservative musical tastes. Of course, these are all fairly broad generalisations, but they help to convey the flavour of the movements. Having said that, this by no means denigrates any of these traditions and what they do because, in most cases, it is effective, but it is difficult to understand why elaborate and frequently expensive costumes and props are necessary to produce the desired results.

This is certainly true of the shamanistic ceremonies where, in addition to a nod towards ritual, substances such as ayahuasca and psilocybin are used to great effect. This brings another factor into play here, the gnostic ideal of achieving spiritual oneness with the cosmos through meditation and other factors comparable with the communion achieved by shamans and Chaos Magicians. Taken a stage further, does this imply that the frequently referred to saints and others of noted piety who achieve ecstatic conditions while meditating upon the nature of God or the sufferings of the crucified Christ are also in a gnostic trance? It is a concept that the Church seems uneasy about discussing, because doing so may serve to undermine its existing doctrines and dogmas regarding spiritual revelations. This should not be the case, but it is, and one would quite reasonably imagine that the seeker after pious illumination and the seeker of gnostic fulfilment would have much more in common, but the inbuilt denial and rejection of anything outside its own narrow interpretation of 'truth' is unacceptable to the Church.

Taken even further, it does seem as though it is an absolute necessity that unshakable and unswerving belief is central to the success of gnostic, ecstatic, shamanic or, indeed, any other kind of trance state, especially if this is achieved by will power alone. This is exactly when belief becomes a magickal tool in its own right and, if this is the case, then there is absolutely no difference regarding the validity of any of these altered states of awareness, because they all achieve an identical sense of union with the divine. Now, what the 'divine' actually means is something else again, but it has to be, indeed must be, the same thing, but viewed from different perspectives. It is unlikely that the Church would consider it in this open-minded manner simply because it is unapproved and, therefore, automatically excluded from its canon of truth. However, the seeker and after gnostic truth and the shaman may have a great deal more in common, because both have considerably less to lose.

As a slight, but possibly still relevant, aside, it also looks as if the same unwavering confidence and belief is an important factor in the non-spiritual world too, especially in the esoteric and rarefied field of quantum physics. In this often-contentious branch of science, it has been demonstrated that the outcome of some experiments can be affected by the inclinations of those conducting them. Might this demonstrate that here is another possible definition of magick and that, in some circumstances, thoughts have the ability to act on the outside world? This nebulous ability is precisely what mages have tried to harness and demonstrate since time immemorial and it was fundamental to the practices of magicians like Aleister Crowley.

Like him or not, there is no doubt that this man was one of the most profoundly influential of all those who regarded themselves as seekers after magickal enlightenment and truth. As briefly mentioned at the beginning, Crowley's doctrine was based on the concept of 'Thelema' or will, which is another way of making the case that an unshakable and instinctive belief in one's action can bring about a change of some kind in line with one's desires. Crowley was also an avowed gnostic, although his techniques to achieve transcendence and contact with the divine latterly took, to put it mildly, a less than wholesome path to get there. As far as Crowley was concerned, he almost certainly regarded himself as a channel for the divine to use as a source of nameless power to further his own needs and ends. If he had been completely successful in his endeavours, then his eventual death in the town of Hastings, in the South of England, would have been a much more eventful and high profile occasion. Interestingly, the concept of an abbey called Thelema first emerged in the 16th Century in the pages of the book called Gargantua, by Francois Rabelais. In one chapter of the book, a monk is honoured for bravery by having an abbey built for him and the monk calls the abbey Thelema. This was no ordinary abbey, though, and it was dedicated to pleasures of the senses, where only the best and most beautiful were allowed. The motto adopted for it is 'Fait Ce Que Vouldras', or 'Do what you will'. Apparently, Crowley had heard of this tale and adapted it to suit his needs.

Oddly enough, and carrying another similarity with Crowley, one other method occasionally employed to achieve unity is the use of so-called Lovecraftian Magick, where the foul, non-human entities dredged from the dark recesses of the mind of the author Howard Phillips (HP) Lovecraft are invoked. We should be very careful here, because there are many who, quite reasonably, insist that these baleful demons have no provenance whatsoever, other than their appearance in the pages of the unsettling tales authored by Lovecraft. Or perhaps the influence is rather more insidious, yet profound, and finds some kind of legitimacy in another of his creations, the grimoire he entitled, The Necronomicon, also known as The Book of Dead Names.

According to Lovecraft's cosmology, eons ago, in the Yemen, an Arab sorcerer, named Abdul Alhazred, allegedly wrote a book of spells and incantations, which supposedly outdid the previously mentioned 'Grimoire of Pope Honorius III' in its evil excesses and notoriety, and an entire system of magick has been created around its supposed contents. These were supposedly pure fiction, although there are a few cognoscenti who insist that what he set down on the page were images of real places and beings drip-fed into his brain by the inhabitants of these realms. One thing that is certain is that the images he created have attained a kind of life quite independent of that imbued into them by Lovecraft. In response to a sizable undercurrent of public demand, two versions of this book were actually produced. One was called The Simon Necronomicon, named after the individual who edited it, and the other one was created by the famous and talented author, Colin Wilson.

It should be pointed out that, as far as I am aware, neither of these men were or are, in any sense, heretical or gnostic, but were simply filling a niche in the market. However, perhaps it goes to show that even a work of fiction may acquire a degree of power if sufficient numbers of people start using it as a source of truth and might this also be the case with the Bible?

Before moving on, we should remember that the words 'heresy' or 'heretic' only means 'choice' or 'one who chooses'. There is nothing sinister or unreasonable in these terms. The unfortunate part came when, after careful consideration, one chose not to embrace Church dogma. Unfortunately, the term, 'heretic', has become hitched to the same wagon as another innocent term, 'occult', which only means hidden, and both of them are now considered as related to magick in all its forms. As an aside, one difference between these two grimoires is the fact that the volume complied by Pope Honorius included pious requests and entreaties for the protection of Almighty God and his angels during the rituals, while Lovecraft's fictitious work had no truck with the traditionally sacred, preferring instead to invoke the denizens of the pit with little thought for the possible consequences.

Chapter 24
Religion and Quantum Physics

As already mentioned in relation to the apparently mathematical nature of the cosmos, there is surely a link here to the strange equations used by physicists in their still ongoing search for the ultimate secret of the universe, the discovery of which would effectively turn human beings into gods. It is here that we are confronted with a very real form of magick and one that the Church might even encourage, because it would finally create an amalgam between science and mysticism. If, for example, the true Holy Grail of science, the 'Unified Field Theory' (UFT), could be expressed as a tiny equation or design yet containing the very stuff of creation itself, might this be the mightiest spell ever created, greater even than the equations devised by Albert Einstein to demonstrate the special theory of relativity and other hitherto unknown truths?

Might it be reasonable to compare sigils with these exotic and esoteric formulae and the spells and incantations used in magickal rites? This concept blends some fascinating, and hitherto unexpected, levels into the enigma. Does it imply that rather than condensing a wish or desire into a sigil using pen and paper, that it would be equally effective if reduced electronically to a line of code on a memory stick or hard drive? On the face of it, this sounds reasonable, but, if that were the case, how would the magician use it and could the whole procedure be made, in effect, automatic, a kind of 'dial a spell'? Or, as may be more likely, does it still require the input of a human being to give direction and purpose to the enterprise? The answer is that no-one knows. It is a facet of magick that has not yet been attempted, but the possibility is tantalising.

There are many people still searching for the ultimate truth, who continually push back the frontiers of science with investigations into genetic engineering and nanotechnology. This time, the results of their experimentation may have a much more deadly outcome, although the Church maintains a silence on the majority these subjects, except for genetic engineering, which it still regards as the sole province of the Almighty. Having said that, if a human being could be cloned or, better still, created from the basic chemicals and building blocks of life, this would surely raise some fascinating ethical and moral questions. Regarding the nature of a clone, if, for example, it did not conform to preconceived intellectual expectations and become, say, a criminal, who would be held responsible, the clone or its donor? Would a clone have any claim on the property of its donor, because keep in mind that the clone is the donor by proxy. Would it have a soul? Would it be the absolute double of the donor? How would it develop intellectually? Would it inherit the genetic traits of its donor or would it have to be programmed? Would it also have to learn and mature through social interaction, example and experience, much as any other flesh and blood human being does?

Now consider the hypothesis of a human being entirely constructed from synthetic DNA. Even though this is currently beyond the capabilities of present day science, the questions become even more far-reaching and worrying. In this case, the person produced would have absolutely no inherited, genetic blueprint to follow, other than that created by its makers. Perhaps this is one branch of science that is a genuine 'no go area'. Perhaps the idea of creating human beings with no inherited genetic traits might be something that the military or some covert government-funded agency would entertain and finance, but is it really something that we would want? To all intents and purposes, these 'people' would be blank, empty canvasses, unless, of course, this branch of science knew which specific genes to alter to produce the kind of being it required. This might even be the worst abuse of science/magick possible. The use of the word, magick, in this context is deliberate, because it begins to directly address the thoughts of Arthur C Clarke on magick and technology as set out in Chapter 2 of this book.

Even if we leave physicists out of the picture, there are many Newtonian scientists who see no dichotomy between their endeavours and a creator God, so they, in a sense, must also embrace the existence of magick. While their discipline and training forces them to reject the ludicrous Creationist mantra that the Earth is approximately six-thousand years old, they still see no problem with a Creator God. However, they base this on the much more reasonable and verifiable basis that, since the entire solar system and the place of the Earth in it seems to be intentional, then this cannot have happened by accident. This paradigm does have a safe and comforting feel to it, but it still opens the door to admit mysticism and magick into their discipline. Evidently, it is easier to accept the possibility that the human race was created, not by some notional God, but through the actions of some interstellar culture seeking to replicate itself. Both of these possibilities have their attractions, but one has profoundly magickal overtones and the other does not. Why should the mystical/magickal one appeal to someone with a rational, materialistic, data-based scientific background, while the other, which applies to neither mysticism nor magick, does not? The only possible answer can be that the mystical solution carries more credibility than the possibility that an extraterrestrial civilisation should even exist, let alone travel the dark and airless void of the cosmos seeding planets as it goes. Strange, perverse even, but true.

What Now?
Nowadays, we can produce synthetic diamonds, not particularly good ones, but, nevertheless, it can be done and the proto-science of alchemy does not exist any longer or, at least, not in the primitive manner of bygone times. As in the Middle Ages with Roger Bacon and John Dee, the modern era has produced its own alchemists and magicians, with pioneers like Lord Rutherford, Albert Einstein, Erwin Schrodinger, Edward Teller and Stephen Hawking *et al* with their research into particle physics, nuclear fission and beyond. Albert Einstein, in particular, introduced concepts in quantum physics that are still reverberating around the scientific community to this day. In fact, many of the implications like 'String Theory' contained in his pioneering equations have had completely unexpected outcomes, outcomes that the great man might have thought unlikely, if not impossible. These are the tantalising hints of time travel, matter transmission and the existence of parallel universes. None of them are practical using our current knowledge of the quantum world, but all that could change with one single flash of insight. This would be the final revelation, when what was once considered magickal became normal and acceptable.

Magicians of The New Age
Another example of apparently magickal techniques being used by the state emerged in the form of experiments funded and endorsed by various intelligence agencies throughout world. This was the attempt to harness supposedly paranormal talents such as 'remote viewing' to enhance their intelligence gathering capabilities, which was regarded as quite separate from the wider implications of such a project. There were certainly no known objections raised by religious bodies over the deployment of such talents, which may either simply be a sign of the times, an instinctive fear of the military machine or a tacit admission that the Church authorities did not judge these abilities as a threat to its own policies.

The reason for this is simple: it was risky enough for those promoting this line of research to approach the hard-headed generals and politicians who control the military budget for financial backing and support without dragging along the considerable negative baggage associated with it, e.g. communication with the deceased and what amounts to fortune telling, along in their wake. The separation had to be convincing and, to some extent, it was, because such a proposal was commissioned and funded in the USA, via the CIA, under the eventual banner of the 'Stargate Project'. In the former USSR, where the bizarre rat race began, it was rather different, because the ethos was dissimilar and, in spite of the aggressive atheism of the communist regime, the Eastern Bloc has always had a much more spiritual culture, although this book will not concern itself with these anomalies, other than to say that, perhaps, the continual oppression created such a need.

However, perhaps this illustrates that we will never be entirely rid of witches and witchcraft, for the imagery is ingrained too deeply in the human psyche where, perhaps, it fulfils a necessary social function and supplies a perceived need for mystical release, a desire to see beyond the mundane and ordinary, to obey a powerful deity, to dare to be different. Although alchemy is still practiced, it is now regarded as an allegorical search for perfection of spirit, almost like a gnostic revelation rather than a method of transmuting metals. Both of these related sciences, although inextricably interwoven, are perceived as quite different, but, as we have seen, they are not and never will be.

Chapter 25
Late Last Night Upon the Stair

Last night I saw upon the stair
A little man who wasn't there
He wasn't there again today
Oh, how I wish he'd go away

William Hughes Mearns (1875-1965)

The above, frequently misquoted, verse is taken from a short poem called *Antigonish*, by William Hughes Mearns, and was originally a whimsical song forming part of a play called *The Psyco-ed* (sic) by the same writer. Its inspiration derives from a reputedly haunted house in the town of Antigonish, situated in Nova Scotia, Canada. The charming little rhyme neatly and succinctly encapsulates the uneasy, and sometimes terrifying, experiences of virtually everyone who has had some form of ghostly encounter.

Visions of madness

Since humanity first walked the Earth, there have been reports of encounters with entities of various kinds that have come to be known alternately as ghosts, revenants, shades, spectres and apparitions etc. These beings do not sit comfortably within the template that human beings have constructed around the attributes associated with humanity. As a race, we instinctively fear them and, in some cases, disguise this fear by rejecting them entirely, preferring instead to deny the evidence of our own senses, even when more than one person shares the vision. Convention attributes such events to 'mass hallucinations' and blames them on aberrations in human perception, such as hysteria and other states of emotional arousal. Disappointingly, any possible psychic attributes are deliberately ignored. So much so that conventional scientific dogma clearly implies that, since these events cannot be evaluated using its parameters, the entities *cannot* exist, which means, according to this logic, that they *do not* exist.

The history of science is littered with examples of this negative paradigm, which is genuinely anomalous, because many of the physicists and scientists specialising in various diverse disciplines reject any possibility of a non-physical life, yet, as we have seen, simultaneously profess to believe in an equally unlikely Creator God - and they see no contradiction in this. A prime example of this comes from the field of genetics where, according to those with religious views, they consider (admittedly with some justification) that the twin spiral of the DNA molecule cannot have come about by millions of evolutionary 'happy accidents'. This, they say, must indicate intelligent design. If human beings could decode and recreate the essence of life itself, does that put them on a par with their notional God and, if so, how would this affect religious belief? It seems, therefore, that belief in the paranormal is acceptable in some cases but not in others and the benchmark relies entirely on what that belief is.

We encountered this earlier in the narrative in a good example of blinkered, joyless and desiccated logic promoted by those who are, by definition, professional debunkers in 17th Century France at the town of Loudon, when an entire convent of nuns displayed signs of apparent demonic possession. Although the story is mainly portrayed by convention as a textbook case of neurotic obsession, the end result of the nuns' actions was the imprisonment, torture and eventual immolation of their confessor, Fr Urbain Grandier, by the Catholic Church. However, bearing in mind that, as we saw, there just might have been a magickal element to at least some of what occurred in the convent, much to their consternation, and in complete defiance of their logic, examples of paranormal phenomena persist in appearing with no rhyme or reason and with no readily discernable pattern.

In the case of the medieval nuns of Loudon, perhaps their concentrated and hyper-intense neurotic ravings actually did produce a form of energy creating weak spots in the veil of reality allowing 'something' to pass through to our side. While there is obviously no proof of this, we must also recall that current interpretations of what occurred all those centuries ago are based entirely on a modern psychiatric theory. On the other hand, these emotions seem remarkably similar to the states of mind induced by certain rituals conducted by shamans and other practitioners of magick as they attempt to summon their familiars, serpents and elementals. The difference here is that, in the case of shamans etc., the invocation is deliberate, but with the nuns it was not. That aside, it is certainly something similar, frequently amplified by the use of natural hallucinogens or other consciousness altering methods, that have, for millennia, permitted shamans to traverse the barrier.

To be fair, it is true that in some cases people do become ill, sometimes seriously so, and really do see things that are not there because the stability of their neural processes has become damaged or confused. In some cases, if the condition is severe enough, the individual is confined to a hospital, both for their own safety and that of the general public. This usually applies to people who act out violent and murderous fantasies under the impression that they are obeying the commands of either a voice that only they can hear or some other unnerving motivating force. Sometimes they can be completely cured through the use of appropriate treatment or, if not cured, the condition can at least be managed through the judicious use of medication.

However, in some of the more extreme cases, it is not uncommon for the sufferer to be kept incarcerated in a secure hospital for the rest of their lives. Do not forget, though, that, even today, in some cases, these unfortunate people would be regarded as 'demon possessed' and have the invading demon brought forth by means of a tub-thumping, Christian fundamentalist, evangelical zealot, frequently making the situation much worse. Make no mistake about it, these blinkered ministries regard everything from toothache to gout as a demonically created disease that will vanish once the 'demon' has been routed.

Tragically, in certain instances where individuals have been released into the community to continue their treatment in the outside world, their supervised 'freedom' has been less than effective and resulted in the murder of innocent people. It is important that we draw points of reference here and apply reality checks, because, if we do not, then anything and everything becomes possible and real. To pursue the line that even the visions of the genuinely insane may be real and valid is to create ripples in the very nature of reality itself, in other words, is reality objective or subjective? Perhaps we can look at this in greater detail when we begin to consider the nature of the walls that contain our own version of reality.

Before moving on, we should, perhaps, recall that, returning once more to Medieval France during the Hundred Years War, a young peasant girl, Jeanne D'arc, better known as St Joan of Arc, also heard 'voices in her head'. These voices were variously attributed to God, St Michael and St Catherine and when the English were about to take Orleans, the terrified and superstitious authorities, on the off chance that she might really have an inside line to supernatural aid, pleaded with her to restore the Dauphine, Charles VII, to the throne and drive the English out. Disguising herself as a man, she was able to convince the government to give her charge of the army and was also advised to appoint a bodyguard.

She did this and, by some weird synchronicity, chose one Gilles de Rais, a man who, as we have seen, was later executed for sorcery and heresy. Bearing in mind that, astonishingly, this woman was not yet twenty years of age, she achieved a great victory for her cause at Orleans, but ended her short life at the stake when she became an annoyance and, more importantly, a thorn in the sides of those whose less than spiritual agendas did not match her own. Remarkably enough, Joan, who was born in 1412, was executed as a witch and heretic a mere twenty-one years later in 1433. Nowadays, she would probably have been diagnosed as schizophrenic, possibly obsessive, prescribed a course of medication and, perhaps, temporarily hospitalised. It can only be wondered whether the paranoid mental states of many charismatic people like Jim Jones, David Koresh and Marshall Applewhite are good examples, all of whom founded destructive cults and other vehicles designed to promote their individual agendas, would stand up to close inspection.

The Role of Religion

It must also surely give one cause to examine the role of religion in the mindset of such individuals and, more importantly, in how they were perceived by those who regarded them as, in some way, 'blessed', 'inspirational' or, in some other way, 'special'. Might this be the same brand of charisma that surrounded the zealots who murdered and maimed in the name of their God? Was it the same certainty with which those who brandished their irrational beliefs as some sort of lure to induce others to join them in their quest? The answer seems to be literally anything, irrespective of how insane, as long as it is done in the name of a God, any God, is acceptable. Does this not give a very genuine cause for concern that religion, or any other irrational belief, can elevate almost anything beyond the pale of common sense, that rationality can be suspended when some unprovable totem is wheeled out and presented as absolute truth and an acceptable reason to murder?

As ever, there are many questions with no ready answers, especially when, particularly in modern times, the state will not speak out or act against superstition, in case it contravenes the politically correct mantras that stifle any possibility of common sense. Indeed, the tail does wag the dog. If true, we, as a culture, should be genuinely afraid, because there will surely come a tipping point and, when that time comes, it will already be too late and our civilisation and culture will slide back into a mind-numbing morass of ignorance, fear and superstition. Paradoxically, it is these same religious ideologies that, while espousing the existence of an all-powerful supernatural being existing outside time and space, will fervently deny the existence of an afterlife, unless it is one that their dogma allows.

Be that as it may, the abilities of those we consider insane or, in some other way, 'different' to discern other levels of reality may be well in advance of those of apparently 'normal' people. Sadly, it may take some time before this is fully realised, because in among the array of the genuinely damaged, there may be a very few whose exquisite psychic sensitivity overwhelms the capacity of their brains to cope with the continuous tsunami of information assailing them. In the case of genuine psychics and mediums, it is possible that, although we all have innate, but latent, psychic abilities, they were probably born with their additional senses already 'switched on' and functioning and they have grown up with it, instinctively learning to filter out what is relevant and what is not. This may not just be a case of 'turning down the volume' for the sake of comfort, either. It might have been for sheer self-preservation.

A look at our own none too distant past reveals much about how society, in the West, at least, regarded those with unusual 'talents' and abilities. In many instances, those with obvious mental problems were regarded as 'outsiders' and, in extreme cases, as agents of evil spirits. In some cases, they were incarcerated by the state in stinking hellholes until they died and the best they or their parents/guardians could hope was that, if they were wealthy enough, they could pay for their unfortunate relative to be cared for in some monastery or other religious institution. Even in Victorian times, the ravings of the insane were frequently the source of depraved amusement for those willing to bribe the ill-trained 'nurses' in the grim, heartless institutions where the insane were housed, to allow them access to the wards. As with 'The Devils of Loudon', once again this was depicted in film, this time in the 1980 work, The Elephant Man, directed by David Lynch, which depicted the tribulations of the shockingly disfigured, but decent and intelligent, John Merrick, the titular Elephant Man. In one scene, a rather brutish warder is shown taking a bribe from sniggering and inebriated sensation seekers, then allowing them to jeer at and torment the unfortunate Merrick.

Thankfully, in the modern, developed world, this attitude has, for the most part, vanished, although the mentally ill still draw curious and wary glances when out in public, but in other less developed cultures, this is not the case. For example, in Indonesia today, in spite of the fact that almost ninety percent of the two-hundred and thirty million population are Muslim, there is still widespread belief in superstition and black magick and psychiatric illness is often associated with demonic possession. This is looked upon as a magickal sickness of the soul or 'sakit jiwa', literally 'soul pain'. It seems odd that the fierce injunctions against non-conformity promoted by Islam cannot totally extinguish the ingrained power of traditional beliefs.

A similar attitude is still prevalent in oil rich Saudi Arabia, where those afflicted with mental illness are hidden well away from the eyes of society. There is an additional issue in this particular country regarding the effective treatment of the mentally ill, the very medications designed to help individual ailments can fall foul of Qur'anic strictures and prohibitions on substances that cause changes in brain function. As a result of this, along with alcohol, they are frequently banned. This anomaly often leads to the relatives of those so afflicted illicitly obtaining the appropriate medicine from neighbouring Bahrain and other bordering countries where, in spite of being Islamic, the same, narrowly-interpreted Wahabist interpretations of Islam do not apply. As an aside, the most commonly prescribed medication among the expatriate community in Saudi Arabia is diazepam, better known as Valium, a popular and relatively inexpensive tranquiliser and muscle relaxant.

Chapter 26
Crossing the Divide

As we have seen, for centuries those who actually witnessed ghostly figures and actually admitted it were thought of as slightly unhinged and sneered at by those who had not yet encountered the pale echoes and revenants of the worlds beyond our own realm. Much the same still occurs today, although there is considerably less stigma attached to it. As we have also seen, it might just be possible that some of those incarcerated in psychiatric institutions may have had genuine sightings and revelations. Unfortunately, with this kind of institutionalised bias, there is no reliable method of independently evaluating the visions or encounters experienced by those held in hospitals. This is a great pity, because the very institutions themselves are reputedly the loci for paranormal activity of all kinds and, in some cases, abundantly so.

This may, once again, resonate with what allegedly occurs among those in enclosed institutions like prisons, convents and monasteries, where sudden outbreaks of hysteria may inadvertently create a weakness in the fabric of reality. If this happens in tightly ordered and controlled environments, especially spiritual ones, where the lifestyle is one of contemplation and meditation, what might the clinically insane be capable of? What horrors, both ancient and modern, might come charging unbidden from the fevered and completely uncensored and uncritical recesses of their subconscious minds and, in particular, the id, that mass of primitive energies that underlies all psychic activity? This must be looked at in one of two ways: the visionaries, whose only 'illness' is a small measure of psychic ability, and those who possess the unfettered raw talent to actually materialise the entities that inhabit the realms existing alongside our own. If, however, those possessing the ability are themselves unable to focus their wild gifts, might those awaiting entry to this world somehow harness this reservoir of psychic energy for their own ends?

As already mentioned, what is the barrier that protects us and our version of what is real? There are several strains of thought on this. One comes from the results of a series of experiments carried out in the picture-book Norfolk village of Scole in the Southeast of England, the results of which were detailed in the book, The Scole Experiment. One particularly revealing experiment strongly suggested that the human race exists in one of several 'layers' of reality. Each layer, which exists in parallel and concurrently with our own, is populated by a variety of entities, including the 'spirits' (surely interchangeable with consciousness) that currently inhabit our bodies and it was with these that the people involved in the Scole experiments communicated. They called them the 'Spirit Team'. According to these discarnate entities, all of the layers contain beings, some corporeal, like us, and some not. Some are aware of the other layers and the beings in them and, once again, some are not. Indeed, some of the entities are fully aware of us, the human race, but are indifferent to us. Perhaps simply because we pose no threat to them or perhaps because what we are is so alien that there are simply no common points of reference.

However, and rather disconcertingly, according to the Spirit Team, one of the layers is populated by a race of non-human beings that are utterly inimical to humanity and would harm us if they could. Why is not entirely obvious, but it may be connected to the fact that we have emotions programmed into us, hate, fear, love, sadness, joy and all the subtle nuances in between. This is what they do not have and they want it and crave it with a greater passion, a greater desire or craving than any drug addict has ever experienced. The Spirit Team, and indeed mediums of my own acquaintance, infer that these particular beings are extraterrestrial when they do actually succeed in migrating to our reality - which they sometimes do – but, in fact, they are not. The only thing that comes close to describing what they might be is the term 'psychic vampires', the name occasionally given to entities that induce absolute terror in human beings in order to slake their debased thirst on the negative emotions produced. Whether this is accurate, or indeed even true, is a matter for debate, but it does at least provide a reason for some of the alleged encounters between human beings and the 'otherworld'. The other point, regarding the nature of the layers and why they can be occasionally breached, hints at the possibility that, in certain, as yet unknown, circumstances, they are permeable.

Of course, quantum physics appears to demonstrate, in its esoteric formulae, the existence of other versions of the universe we live in and, make no mistake about it, these other versions of reality are not small, convenient, neatly-packaged, self-contained slivers, they are full-sized, actual functioning universes in their own right. This is what particle physics theorises is alongside us in what they call 'D-brane' (membrane) universes and our own universe is but one membrane among all the others. This is quite a concept, but, nevertheless, it is the only one that resonates with the mediumistic concept of separate realms inhabited by both physical entities and non-corporeal beings. In fact, the idea is also demonstrated in the faith-based concept that, upon death, we are segregated into the good and the bad, judged upon how well we have conducted ourselves in life and then assigned a position in one of several layers of non-physical existence.

The worse the person was in life, the lower down they are placed and only after expiating their misdeeds can they progress to the upper layers. Those on a higher level can travel to the levels below, but not the other way round.

There is no get out clause here and, according to some strains of mediumistic belief, that is how it works. The idea, of course, has direct comparisons with the Roman Catholic concept of 'Purgatory', where the souls of the dead who are not adjudged ready to arrive in Heaven are placed until they have 'served their time', so to speak, and become purged of sin, hence 'purgatory'. The Church also had another subdivision of Purgatory called 'Limbo', which was thought necessary because children who died either in the womb, at birth or very shortly after and had not received the sacrament of baptism would have died with the stigma of original sin upon them and gone to Hell.

This fate was, entirely appropriately, considered most judgemental and unfair, so, after much theological chin stroking and due consideration, the idea of limbo was scrapped and children who die, even with original sin upon them, are now assumed to go straight to Heaven. The entire concept seems quite arbitrary and bizarre and may reflect the manner in which religious beliefs of any persuasion attempt to rationalise imponderables and still remain within the rules of its own dogma. Predictably, various ultra-conservative factions within the Church do not approve and, in their own way, are as grim and joyless as the atheists and rationalists.

Is this brief diversion relevant? Yes, it is, because it helps demonstrate just how entire cosmologies are built with varying degrees of validity around a range of beliefs, in this case, religious as opposed to scientific. How then can we interact (if at all) with these alternate realities and remain at least within touching distance of sanity, how can we catch glimpses into it and, perhaps even, interact with it? Strangely enough, scientists and physicists who espouse religious belief are fully aware that their respective areas of study inevitably continue to demystify subjects formerly the sole provenance of the supernatural. When faced with problems that they cannot yet explain, there must be a great temptation to attribute them, whatever they are, to 'God's work' and, as such, automatically magickal and beyond human understanding. This must result in them having to continually reset and redefine their horizons in order to continue with the comfort of belief in a Creator God.

Defining the Barriers
In my opinion, one of the best analogies for the parallel universe hypothesis comes from the unlikely quarter of video gaming and the occasional defects called 'glitches' that can crop up in the games. These 'glitches' are faults in the game programming and when the developers find them, usually after the game has been released, they create downloadable 'patches' to rectify the original defects. So, how do the glitches affect the games and are they relevant to parallel dimensions and realities? The answer is yes. Consider this: in one extremely popular console game, *Call of Duty: World at War*, it was possible to leave the game map in which the action takes place and move around the

outside looking in and still be able to affect the internal game play. In another example of this popular game, when played online, the player was able to literally step inside a wall or crawl around in the sky while shooting at the other participants. The game developers may now have rectified these glitches, but the game players seem adept at finding new ones.

Staying with this analogy introduces an interesting concept. Might it be conceivable that the human race is an imperfect programme, with each and every human being playing their individual role? If our 'programmers' had got it right at the beginning, then our race and civilisation would probably have been as perfect (or, indeed, imperfect) as our creators/programmers intended. Since we are manifestly not perfect, far from it, might our 'inventors' have recognised this and the various prophets who have appeared over the years have been the equivalent of the 'patches' used to repair defects in a computer programme? Stranger yet, might the occasional sorcerer or magician who appears from time to time also be flaws in the programme that attempt to manipulate it for their own purposes? After all, if we participate in the programme, then in an echo of Arthur C Clarke and his insightful comments about technology, any changes would appear as magick.

Could this be the manner in which reality is created and what we consider to be real is only as solid as the writers of the programme make it and are there unintended 'glitches' in there just waiting to be exploited? This being the case, might outside entities be able to exploit the glitches for their own ends and physically interact with us and does this mean that they are aware that reality is only a programme and simply took advantage the imperfections? Do mediums and psychics inadvertently detect and use the glitches to communicate with the 'departed'? Well, perhaps, but there is another, even more exciting, possibility that we shall consider a little later. Yes, many questions, but the answers now seem tantalisingly close, are we, once again, considering the possibility of a Matrix-like version of cyberworlds, where reality is nothing more than a self-replicating programme with inherent defects or is this perhaps a supposition too far? What is reality? Is it how we actually perceive it or, in a parallel with the UFO phenomenon, does it shape itself to our expectations of what should be there? This concept resonates with an idea floated by some quantum physicists who, neatly dovetailing with the findings of the Scole group, consider that reality is but one of countless probabilities existing as 'waves' that only snap into being when a decision is made. They equate reality with collapsed 'probability waves'.

Before considering this in more depth, perhaps we should consider just how we, as human beings, actually catch glimpses of what lies in the other side. There has been much speculation that all children are natural mediums. Traditionally, this has been attributed to the assumption that, since the minds of children are less cluttered with preconceptions and doubt than adults, they may be more open and amenable to contact with what adults might reject or ignore out of hand. It is now known that the brains of children up to the ages of six or seven, and sometimes a little older, exist naturally in the alpha and theta state (approx 7.85Hz and 4-7Hz respectively), which are the brain wave frequencies usually conducive to psychic experiences. This means that children are permanently 'switched on' to signals that adults are no longer equipped to receive, unless induced while in a meditative state.

This explanation has been used to demonstrate why many children have 'invisible friends' that are totally invisible and inaudible to adults. It is a common phenomenon that countless parents have observed in their youngsters. The only time that adults regularly experience the alpha state without meditation is while they are in the process of falling asleep. Crucially, this is the very time when they experience what psychiatrics style (or perhaps 'dismiss' would be more appropriate) as 'Hypnagogic Hallucinations'. This description may well be another method by which conventional science attempts to marginalize experiences that it does not fully understand by herding them into manageable, stable and easily-definable limits and names. It is also another example of how rationality defends itself by declaring alternate interpretations as unworthy of consideration.

Media-friendly psychologists, psychiatrists, stage magicians and illusionists often adopt this ploy when they participate in TV documentaries designed to demonstrate that paranormal encounters are invariably explained by either mundane and misinterpreted natural occurrences or chicanery. Their 'evidence' is rarely, if ever, refuted or challenged and it might be instructive to see just how the rationalists would fare when made to justify their cast-iron 'proofs'. This reticence is never shown to those whose beliefs challenge orthodoxy, simply because it does not make for good 'entertainment'. The word, 'entertainment', is crucial here, because, in the United Kingdom at least, the broadcasting regulations forbid the subjects of paranormal phenomena or mediumship to be presented as fact, they must come under the heading of entertainment.

On the other hand, religious broadcasting is allowed to proceed unhindered and unchallenged as an established fact with no hard evidence to back it up, which demonstrates the level of institutionalised hypocrisy surrounding the subject. To be fair, though, there are individuals within the ranks of orthodoxy who do not always share the narrow conventions of their colleagues and physicists expressing broad agreement with my own hypotheses regarding alternate realities have, in the past, contacted me. While expressing their support, they cannot, indeed dare not, 'go public', in case they incur the jibes and mockery, if not downright rejection, by their colleagues and I have no desire to see a career 'crash and burn' through the intolerance of others.

Another curious adjunct to children and alpha waves is the existence of the enigmatic pineal gland within the human brain. In the case of children, this small, almond-sized organ, which is located in the brain where the spinal chord terminates, is active and, upon puberty, slowly begins to calcify. The pineal gland has long been associated with the so-called 'third eye', the hypothetical organ in the middle of the forehead that allegedly permits glimpses into the invisible realms. The pineal is the only source of the hormone, melotonin, in the body and is also receptive, via the nervous system, to the light seen through the eye. This is normally cited by the New Age movement as proof of the existence of the 'third eye', but is more likely to be a misinterpretation of the function of the pineal, although the Egyptians regularly celebrated it by depicting it as the uraeus snake seen on the brow of Pharaonic headwear. Quite how they knew this is, like many ancient mysteries, not fully understood, but it may be rooted in ancient traditional knowledge concerning the seven alleged 'chakras' (or sites of spiritual significance) situated in the human body. Melotonin is only produced in darkness, i.e. at night, and is vital to the functioning of the body clock and immune system. If produced in large enough quantities, in common with other neurotransmitters, it can and does produce altered states of consciousness and 'visions'. If, however, there is a valid connection between the pineal and psychic ability, then, since it is most active in children, this, along with the alpha state, surely suggests that children, all children, are potential psychic prodigies.

There is yet another possible factor here and that is the function of REM (Rapid Eye Movement) sleep and how this may directly affect the production of alpha waves in the brain. It is a scientific fact that, if one closes one's eyelids and elevates one's eyes to approximately twenty degrees, alpha waves are triggered automatically. This entirely natural phenomenon is exploited during the treatment of some mild psychiatric disorders when the patient is encouraged to perform the actions required to create alpha waves. A comparatively recent and worthwhile development of this effect is in the treatment of Post Traumatic Stress Disorder (PTSD) in veterans returning from war zones and others who have experienced dramatic, life-changing events.

This begs the question, if the eyes are moving around in REM sleep, is it not possible that they will attain the necessary degree of inclination to bring on the alpha state and, in doing so, induce 'psychic' experiences? Could this be another explanation for hypnagogic and hypnopompic visions and might they not, after all, be a random product dredged from the imagination? This is obviously not a concept that would be warmly welcomed by the medical profession, who would doubtless insist on carrying out an array of tests and evaluations, whose outcomes, should they not agree with their preconceptions, be rapidly hidden from view. Since it is also an established fact that the unborn child in the womb spends approximately eighty percent of the time in an alpha state, might it be possible that a form of 'programming' is taking place? Might information be passed directly into the brain of the developing foetus, where it is filed and stored away for later use, or might this information be encoded elsewhere? Could this information emerge, unbidden, in the abilities of those who are able to commune with the invisible world?

The DNA Bridge

We are, each and every one of us, composed of billions of DNA molecules and, when these molecules are microscopically examined, they take the form of graceful spirals containing all that makes us what we are and, perhaps, it is this very structure that opens links between realities, the 'magickal realms'. Although our scientists have unravelled much of the coding of this molecule, there is still much about it that they do not understand and, as such, have labelled that for which they can find no use or is duplicated as 'Junk DNA'. Now, in line with the rationalists and debunkers, who state that paranormal phenomena does not happen simply because it cannot happen, we find the same reaction in microbiology, because, in this discipline, since a use cannot be found for the superfluous DNA, there is no use for the DNA.

One view regarding the physical structure of DNA suggests that it might act as an antenna of some kind, but to receive what kind of signal? Might it be the very molecular structure of our physical makeup that is the key to the mystery of telepathy and contact with the 'otherworld'? The one slight hitch here is the fact that brainwave activity can be measured as it reacts to stimuli or various kinds. It is how we are able to determine that the brain enters a range of electrical states as we move through various stages of consciousness. Does this suggest that the brain, rather than acting as the complete communication device, is the processing unit for messages sent from the DNA? This notion, although not easy to grasp, would actually make more sense. The issue here is, monitoring the DNA concurrently with the tests being conducted, what would be the relevant indictors that a change had occurred and how would it be determined that the change was 'psychic', as opposed to another function, these are the protocols required.

While explaining the mechanism by which we may achieve communication with the additional realities is one thing, perhaps it is more of a one-way street than we care to admit. By and large, the communication, in a physical sense, at least, seems to emanate mainly from the invisible 'other side', while the best we are apparently able to achieve is the ability to communicate by non-conventional, i.e. 'psychic', means. There have been attempts to explain how this works that seem to draw comparisons with radio transmitters and the transmission of thoughts as a form of, albeit subtle, electromagnetic radiation. This might be true, but there is another possible explanation involving the very nature of our being, the fact that we consist entirely of subatomic particles.

Fortunately, this is not speculation, it is a fact. If our bodies contain, as previously mentioned, material from the earliest spectral flare in the cosmos and if the quantum phenomenon of non-locality is also true, as it seems to be, because quantum entanglement has been demonstrated more than once, then we are at one with the universe and all it contains. That being the case, then our bodies link with everything in the cosmos, which means that the DNA comprising our bodies also contains these ancient particles. The only conclusion possible is that since non-locality is a fact and sibling particles communicate with one another, irrespective of how far apart they are, then this may, indeed, be how communication is achieved and DNA acts as the antenna. The twin subjects of the nature of the universe and that of reality have been sources of considerable philosophical debate for millennia - that and the possibility that the universe might, after all, be the result of deliberate action.

One outcome of this might be that, given enough time, the religionists of all persuasions may finally come to admit that what they have been preaching for millennia may be more fundamental than cherry-picked sections of 'truth' they have been presenting as the only way to achieve redemption and union with the divine. They have persistently refused to accept the legitimacy of any other way than their own and, in the past, took rigorous steps to ensure that any upstart belief was strangled before it took root and posed a threat to its supremacy. But now things are changing, caused in no small measure by the gradual decimation of monotheism as the only belief of choice, and if there is no accommodation, the end is in sight for Christianity and, perhaps even, for Judaism. Islam still has some way to go, because its edicts are still enforced by the kind of sanctions that were once part and parcel of the hysteria, fear and unthinking religious conformity of the Middle Ages.

Unfortunately, Islam is still in the process of evolving, much as Christianity had to. The difference is that the Islamic zealots and fanatics have 21st Century weapons to enforce their conservative dogmas and beliefs and will use them. Islam, too, has its mystical side in Sufism and it also had its sorcerers and necromancers as well, who, likewise, explored the dark side of magick, although the accounts of what they achieved are nowhere near as high profile as the Black Magicians who used the ancient tenets of Christianity and Judaism as a springboard. Hopefully, one day, all of the artificial barriers will drop and the human race will awaken to a joyous epiphany of realisation and see that magick is real and it is part of the natural world. Who knows, it might even be the day that we finally become the means of our own salvation.

Epilogue
The Final Word: A Warning

Authors work in a variety of ways, but whatever method the individual chooses, in the end, it amounts to whatever works best and, in this instance, the background research for this book required that I immerse myself in the subject of magick. The research almost became an obsession, so let this serve as a warning to anyone who seeks to dabble in this frequently dangerous area, because the subject can have a deep, lasting and not always desirable effect on vulnerable individuals. In my own case, what happened was, indeed, undesirable, but, on reflection, not entirely unexpected, having had a similar experience some years previously. While writing a section of the original manuscript dealing with the Black Mass and those who celebrate it, I began experiencing sensations of profound unease, accompanied by flashes of deep, bone-chilling cold.

This situation went on for a few days, but I tried to ignore it, putting it down to a mixture of imagination and the gloomy and depressing nature of the subject matter. However, the situation came to a head in the early hours of the morning, just as I was completing this section, when my wife and I were awoken from our sleep by the sound of something moving around the house - something large! The sounds took the form of scratching, scraping and bumps and they came from all around us with our bedroom as the focus. The sounds initially emanated from behind the plasterboard, then the ceiling and, finally, within the room itself.

For the first time in my life, I was genuinely concerned and my wife was too alarmed to put the light on for fear of what might be there. We lay there in the semi-dark for around thirty minutes as the sounds continued with no interruption. Then, at around 3:30am, as the daylight slowly increased in intensity, the sounds gradually diminished in frequency and volume until they finally stopped altogether. Only then did my wife and I manage to fall into a restless sleep. The following morning, after my wife had gone out, I stood in the empty house and asked whatever had been there to please leave, as there was no point in it remaining. Fortunately, it heeded my request and there were no more episodes. I want to make clear that we live close by a river in a house first built in 1785 and, as such, we have had the odd mouse on previous occasions, but what happened was not caused by any mouse, or rat, for that matter. I have heard both and know the difference. I am not ashamed to admit that, as I lay in bed that night, I felt a cold dread clutch at me. I was literally paralysed with fear, as if some atavistic instinct warned me not to move.

The only other time that something similar has occurred was after I attended an exorcism, or 'cleansing', as they are now called in these politically-correct times. The exorcism had been conducted (successfully, I might add) in a small hotel, a few miles from my home, and, in the process of the ceremony, I had somehow attracted an unwanted entity to me and it had followed me home. It expressed itself as an appalling stench, tightly contained in a small area inside the living room of my house. My wife noticed it immediately (no-one could miss it), but did not know its cause at that time, but I, on the other hand, had a good idea of its nature. I made every effort to remove it by opening all the windows and doors, allowing a breeze to blow though the house, but all this did was cause it to move into the kitchen. Eventually, in spite of my best efforts, it was still there, so, after two days, I waited until my wife had gone out one evening to baby-sit and I stood in the house and asked it to leave. Once again, it did. The strange thing is that it went immediately and there was no transition. It was like turning off a switch. One moment it was there and the next it had gone. Like the most recent manifestation, it did not return either.

There is one other occurrence worth mentioning here and, once again, it involved an exorcism, this time involving a thirty-year-old male, who had, through no fault of his own, become possessed by the spirit of a younger man who had been murdered in a drunken brawl. The possessing entity was evidently intensely misogynistic and took a dislike to the man's partner and made her life unpleasant in a number of ways, including physical attacks where blood was drawn. The outcome of the unfortunate series of events was an exorcism (which, as we have seen, is a type of magick) to remove the possessing entity. The ritual began in a typically low key fashion and those present (five in total, including the possessed man) felt a gradually escalating impression of increasing 'pressure'. A suitable analogy is the sensation experienced immediately prior to a thunderstorm. Then there was a brief hiatus and a feeling of calm, rather like the eye of the storm. This did not last for long, though, and when the entity finally departed, every open door in the entire house simultaneously slammed shut. This happened around nine years ago and, so far, there have been no further occurrences.

There are a number of reasons for sharing this with you, but mainly because, unless you are confident about what you are doing, do not get involved with magick, but, if you feel that you can, then be prepared for some adverse outcomes. Always remember that these entities do not have to go (or, by the same token, come), but, since they need us to get here, failure to comply with our wishes means that they may not be allowed to return. Another point to emphasise is that it is important to recognise that they are real and they exist and, vitally, to let them know this, which can usually be sufficient to encourage them to depart. I suppose it is reasonable to liken this to a 'banishing' or, yes, an exorcism, but on a much lesser scale.

I can only assume that my focussed research into the darker side of magick had inadvertently opened a 'doorway' by amplifying my own, largely dormant, abilities, which allowed this entity to slip though. I do realise that I have a degree of psychic ability that was ignited through my long-term interest in paranormal and occult subjects, involving long periods of contact with mediums and psychics. It is contact with these talented people that frequently 'open up' the abilities that lie unused in the majority of human beings. These are the same people who, in previous and less enlightened times, would have been feared and possibly executed as sorcerers, witches and warlocks. If you, the reader, still feel inspired to carry out your own investigations and experiments into these subjects, then, at least, you have been warned.

END

Appendices

A list of incense related recipes

For the interest of the reader, I have included a list of natural preparations that can be used as incense for a variety of purposes, ranging from purification to intoxication. However, if anyone does decide to use them, I cannot guarantee the results or any possible side-effects that they may have, so, as they say, 'on your head be it'. Please also note that many of these ingredients, where obtainable, are, at present, also legal highs, but some are definitely not (and I am not too sure about the efficacy of rabbit dung).

Please note that, due to their ingredients, some of these incenses have very obvious hallucinogenic properties and great care should be taken when using them. Ideally, they should be used in circumstances where there is at least one other person present who has not either inhaled them or taken any other kind of consciousness-altering substance, including alcohol.

Bodhanath Incense

Thoroughly dry and mix equal parts:

Indian juniper, Balu, Pama and Shupa.
Sprinkle incense onto glowing charcoal embers.

Conjuring Spirits Incense

Thoroughly dry and mix:

1 part Salu Henbane
1/4 part cinnamon bark
1/4 part coriander seed
1/4 part fennel root or seed
1/4 part olibanum

Using a mortar and pestle or even a coffee grinder, grind the ingredients into a fine powder and sprinkle incense on to glowing charcoal embers. If using a domestic coffee grinder, please clean it and wash it out thoroughly or, if in any doubt, scrap it.

Hadra" Asthma Incense

Hadra was once available in pharmacies throughout Europe to treat asthma attacks. The ingredients are still known, but their proportions are not.

Ingredients: Cannabis indica, Datura stramonium, Hyoscyamus niger, Lobelia inflata, Eucalyptus, Saltpeter, Menthol oil.

Hecate Incense

Thoroughly dry and mix equal parts:

Coriander seed, Hemlock root, Henbane, Laurel leaf, Myrrh, Oilbanum, Opium resin, Sandalwood, Storax and Syrian rue seed.

Sprinkle the incense onto glowing charcoal embers.

Incense for Divining the Future

Thoroughly dry and mix equal parts:

Olibanum, Psilocybe cubensis or Psilocybe semilanceata, Salvia Divinorum and a pinch of Parsley root.

Sprinkle incense onto glowing charcoal embers. Note that three of the ingredients are natural hallucinogens.

Incense for Leaving That Which Is Hidden Unknown

Thoroughly dry and mix equal parts:

Celery seed, Coriander seed, Henbane, Opium poppy and Saffron.

Add freshly-pressed hemlock juice to the mixture and sprinkle the incense onto glowing charcoal embers.

Mongolian Purification Incense

Thoroughly dry and mix equal parts:
Juniper branch, Sade tree, Silver fir, Wild thyme.
Sprinkle incense onto glowing charcoal embers.

Mongolian Shaman Incense

Thoroughly dry and mix equal parts:

Juniper branch, Rabbit dung and Wild thyme.

Grind the ingredients into a fine powder and sprinkle incense onto glowing charcoal embers.

"Pressant" Asthma Incense

Thoroughly dry and mix parts:

4 parts Datura stramonium
3 parts Saltpeter
1 1/2 parts Gum arabic
1 part Cannabis indica
1/4 part Hyoscyamus niger
1/5 part Anethol

Sprinkle incense onto glowing charcoal embers. Smoke is to be inhaled to subdue asthma attacks. I suspect that the inclusion of the datura and cannabis may serve to induce some kind of mild, trance-like state.

Roman Incense

Thoroughly dry and mix equal parts:

Laurel leaf, Juniper branch, Vervain, Salvia Officinalis and Thyme.

Sprinkle incense onto glowing charcoal embers.

Spirit-Herb Incense

Thoroughly dry and mix equal parts:

Celery, Coriander seed,and Hemlock root.

Sprinkle incense onto glowing charcoal embers.

Tarahumara Ritual Incense

Thoroughly dry and mix equal parts:

Copal and Peyote.

Grind the ingredients into a fine powder and sprinkle incense onto glowing charcoal embers.

A List of Grimoires

Another list that might be of interest is this one concerning the various grimoires that abound. Please remember, however, that, as with the previous list of incenses, no guarantees can be made about their accuracy, effectiveness or ability to harm. Also be warned that, as has been seen in my own case, using them, reading them or even involving oneself in this subject can have profound and undesirable side-effects. However, they are added here to allow any interested readers further sources of original information. It has to be said that most of these works are based on **pseudepigraphical** texts, which means that they stem from Jewish writings dating from around the 1ˢᵗ Century BC to the 1ˢᵗ Century AD. These texts were supposedly divinely revealed, and this includes the works of magick, but they were not included in the Greek contributions to the Old Testament. In the traditions of the Roman Catholic Church, these works are described as 'apocryphal' and the meaning is exactly the same. All of this censorship was repeated during the Council of Nicea in AD 325 when the New Testament was created and whatever did not fit, or was doctrinally inconvenient or deemed 'unsound', was rejected.

Speaking purely for myself, of those works of magick that I have seen, I did not find any of them particularly easy to read nor immediately understandable, because much of the content is written in an archaic manner which demands very careful study. The texts also assume a pre-existing working knowledge of the subject and complete acceptance of magick as a fact. Perhaps this is deliberate and designed to protect the curious and the innocent from harm. That said, these grimoires are works of immense, latent power and should be used with extreme care.

Be aware that this list is far from complete and there are many other quasi-magickal works around that are derived from the books mentioned. There will probably be those who will argue with what is set out below, which is acceptable, because there is still a great deal of confusion about these books stemming from the fact that the later ones freely use the material in the earlier ones. There is also confusion about the differences between the grimoires attributed to King Solomon and the separate books that comprise them. However, the works detailed below are considered the fountainhead of inspiration for all those that followed.

The Key of Solomon the King: This is probably the first serious attempt at creating a book of magickal practices and is concerned with the means by which King Solomon built his fabled temple in Jerusalem using the services of some forty demons. He obtained this demonic aid through the power of a ring given to him by the archangel, Michael. The ring was in the form of a pentagram inscribed with the secret name of God (*the actual Seal of Solomon*) and Solomon, through the use of various guiles, managed to imprint this name on the prince of the demons, Beelzebub or Beelzebul. This done, the rest of the demons were compelled to obey his commands. Solomon also learned that, at one time, Beelzebub was the highest ranking of all the angels before his expulsion from Heaven. Another purpose for this tome appears to be in the quest for hidden treasure and influencing the thoughts of others. Although this grimoire claims to have been written by none other than King Solomon himself, it is unlikely, because it did not appear in print until sometime between the 1st and 5th Centuries AD, which was almost a thousand years after the death of King Solomon and the completion of his temple. Some sources have described it as pompous nonsense.

The Lesser Key of Solomon', also called 'The Lemegeton: This appeared circa 1641. The work comprises a number of books that, together, form the *Lemegeton*, one of which is *The Goetia*. The word, 'goetia', means howling and describes the way in which the magician screams the words of the invocations and also deals with the manner in which demons can be invoked and of their rank and abilities. Another is the *Theurgia-Goetia*, one of the definitions applied by the Church, and applies to the spirits of the cardinal points of the compass. Then there is the *Pauline Art* (there is no obvious meaning for 'Pauline Art', but it may be a reference to the writings of St Paul and the Pauline Gospel, upon which much of Roman Catholic doctrine is based), which is used to control the angels associated with the day and night and it is also used in reference to the Zodiac. The remaining two volumes are *Almadel Art,* which identifies four separate ranks of spirits while *Ars Notoria* or *Notorious Art* refers to something similar, but with potentially dangerous side-effects. Like almost all the grimoires, *The Lesser Key of Solomon* requires that the magician observe strict rules of cleanliness and purity in thought and deed and that the information it contains should not be knowingly used to harm others.

The Sword of Moses: This is a grimoire of Hebrew magick compiled and edited around 1865 by one Moses Gaster, using 14th Century source documents (although they might be much earlier, some accounts give the date as 400AD). The 'sword' is not a physical artefact made of metal, but comprises a series of invocations using the names of 'angels'. Five of these names are: Cqd, Huzi, Mrgizial, Uhdrziulu and Tutrisi, and I have no idea how they are pronounced, although, perhaps, that is a deliberate ploy to ensure the names are not misused.

Picatrix: Also known as the *Ghayat al Hakim'* or *The Aim of the Wise* appeared in 1256 and may well be the most important book ever written on astrological magick. This grimoire is an enormous and highly detailed work and is considerably larger than most other contemporary works on magick. Parts of the work appear to reflect elements of techniques used by Aleister Crowley and it describes one so called 'confection', comprising blood, brains and urine. Crowley was also given to offering his followers similarly disgusting items that he dubbed 'love cakes' and were made of faeces, blood and other ingredients. This is hardly surprising, though, because Crowley was an avid collector and compiler of magickal techniques from any and every source and would adopt and adapt whatever he felt was relevant to his own canon of magick. The work was first translated into Latin in 1256 for the Castilian king, Alfonso the Wise.

Pseudomonarchia Daemonum: Roughly translated as *The False Hierarchy of Demons* and published in 1563 is a list of sixty-nine demons, which form most of the *Goetia*, although the *Goetia* numbers the demons at seventy-two, which is, of course, a number with great magickal significance. A partial list of the demons mentioned in the *Pseudomonarchia Daemonum* is as follows: Marbas, Pruflas, Amon, Barbatos, Buer, Gusoin, Zepar, Beleth, Sitri, Belial, Paimon, Astaroth, Malphas, Murmur, Balaam and Phoenix. Some familiar and some less so and some, believe it or not, the names given to some extraterrestrial visitors by old school 'contactees'. This, if true, gives rise to some fascinating speculation about either the information provided by those recording these events or the nature of the entities themselves. More worryingly, the name, Balaam, has also been attributed to Christ, in one apocryphal account, when he is referred to as 'Balaam the Lame'.

Dee's Five books of Mystery: (1581-83) Dr John Dee, a brilliant polymath and, among other things, an alchemist and the traditional source of the Enochian system of magick. He also invented the curious system of writing (or code) that was supposedly the means by which Dee and his assistant, Kelley, communicated with the Enochian 'Angels' that feature in much of his writing. Careful study of what is written about these entities reveals that they were probably not angels in any conventional sense.

The Book of the Sacred Magick of Abra-Melin the Mage: This grimoire dates from the mid-15th Century and tells of the teachings of an Egyptian mage, Abra –Melin, as recounted by a German Jew, Abraham of Worms. It describes a form of powerful, but relatively peaceful, Kabbalistic magick and features prominently in both the practices of The Hermetic Order of The Golden Dawn and in the system of Thelemic magick espoused by Aleister Crowley. Perhaps we should consider that the Kabbala forms part of most early systems of magick and, in its original form, at least, was written in Hebrew. It has been claimed by some factions within Judaism that this was the language spoken by angels and it was the first language ever used by human beings and, because of this, is inherently magickal, although this would obviously depend on both the era and context.

The Black Pullet: This 18th Century book of magickal practices concentrates on the use of talismans, but also encompasses necromancy (a magickal system that involves invoking the spirits of the dead) and the almost ubiquitous system of spiritual teachings, the Kabbala. Although it teaches a variety of techniques, the grimoire can also be used to produce the titular 'Black Pullet', which, in this instance, becomes the hen that laid the golden egg. This is a concept that crops up in various folk tales and traditions. The book also contains the method of producing such a marvellous creature and involves having a hen hatch one of its own eggs, but kept blindfold during the hatching process and it should also be kept in a box lined with black material. The resultant hatchling should be able to detect the presence of hidden gold, so at least this element of the story is consistent. The work has also been associated with another text known as the *Red Dragon* (see *The Grand Grimoire*).

Grimoire of Pope Honorius III (1670): A notorious and well-known black magick grimoire, allegedly created by Pope Honorius III and incorporating ideas drawn from earlier works. Noted by the magician, Eliphas Levi, as the most evil book on magick ever published and, given the nature of the other grimoires, that is quite a claim. The book itself deals with the invocation of rebellious angels by means of necromancy. Actually, although necromancy is widely known (and used), it can also be associated with some techniques associated with spiritualist mediums and is one of the reasons that that mediums and psychics are sometimes mistrusted and feared.

Le Petit Albert: Another 19th Century grimoire named after the alchemist and proto-scientist, Albertus Magnus, that makes use of the ever-useful Kabbala and other forms of 'natural magick'.

Grimorium Verum (1817):
A grimoire devoted to the Black Mass and other related subjects that draws much from *The Key of Solomon*. This particular work is quite open about its function in that it makes clear that it is primarily designed to 'summon devils'.

Although purporting to be one volume, in reality, it is divided into two sections. The first is the *Grimorium Verum* itself, which gives the would-be magician instructions on how to prepare for the invocation. This includes such specific details as how to make the paper on which sigils and signs are to be drawn, as well as the methods by which to invoke and banish the spirits. The second part contains the so-called 'admirable secrets' of Albertus Magnus, the 'Petit Albert' in the title of the previous grimoire. Interestingly, the volume is not wholly demonic in nature and some sections might be classified as 'white magick'.

Le Grand Grimoire (circa 1845): A latter day grimoire dealing with black magick, which derives much from the already mentioned *Black Pullet* and most of the earlier works of magick. It might be regarded as a distillation of all the rest and, due to one of its workings, is sometimes referred to as the *Red Dragon*.

Modern variants

The Necronomicon: This is described earlier in the text and, although derived from the writings of Howard Phillips Lovecraft, achieved a richly deserved life of its own and, as also already mentioned, there is a strain of magick devoted to the cosmology he created. This originally fictitious work was elaborated upon and actually written by other authors, but is largely inspired by Sumerian mythology and the *Ars Goetia*, which is a section in *The Lesser Key of Solomon*. Appropriately enough, and given the nature of what Lovecraft wrote about, this work concerns summoning demons.

Magick in Theory and Practice: This influential grimoire by Aleister Crowley is probably one of the more accessible works on this extremely esoteric subject. It outlines his ideas on what magick is and how it works. It also sets out the manner in which the rituals should be performed, the wording of the spells and incantations and the style of dress that should be adopted. Some of it's (and therefore Crowley's) concepts were incorporated into the rituals of The Order of The Golden Dawn.

The Book of The Law: Another magickal work produced by the ever inventive and prolific mage, Aleister Crowley. In this work, he sets out his recognition of the power in the feminine principle and also the manner in which his system of magick (Thelema/Will) worked. As with *Magick in Theory and Practice*, it is also fairly accessible to the newcomer, mainly because the language used is much less archaic (if a trifle pompous). It is also a prime example of the use of Ritual Magick.

The Voynich Manuscript: The creator of this bizarre document is unknown and the reason for writing it equally so and it is, perhaps, the most enigmatic of all the works that might function as a grimoire. Its text and many illustrations of seemingly unknown plants have never been deciphered and it may even be a centuries-old hoax. Nevertheless, it just might be a magickal treatise as well or a work devoted to alchemy or even gnosis, but encoded in such away that those who have so far tried to decode it, and there have been several attempts, have met with failure.

An alternate explanation theorises that it most definitely is not a hoax nor is it a grimoire, but it is, instead, a handwritten account and travelogue, much in the style of many early explorers who wrote painstaking journals detailing their travels to foreign lands and what they encountered there. Think of it on the lines of the journals of Charles Darwin when he set sail aboard the Beagle. Might this manuscript be the account of some early psychonaut or magician leaving a log of his encounters? So far, there is no consensus as to what it really represents and, at present, there the matter rests.

The Satanic Bible: This influential work, produced by Anton Szandor LaVey, the founder of the Church of Satan, might also qualify as a grimoire of sorts, although it seems more concerned with the personal philosophy and lifestyle (magickal and otherwise) adopted by LaVey. That said, it does include a series of incantations designed to invoke specific entities and effects. The ideology of LaVey (two of whose acolytes were the film star, Jayne Mansfield, and entertainer, Sammy Davis Junior) appears to have been dedicated to hedonism rather than the operation of magickal rites. There does not seem to be a great deal of available evidence for any effective magickal workings achieved by The Church of Satan.

The Strangest Grimoire of All - The Holy Bible
Perhaps the ultimate heresy, and one that transcends all types of Christian belief, involves one of the best-selling volumes of all time, which may also be the most widely-read grimoire of them all. I refer, of course, to the Holy Bible in all its versions, translations and traditions. It only requires a slight change in perception and paradigm to see the Bible for the immense treasure trove of magick that it really is, but this fresh interpretation of what it contains has been rendered unthinkable by its adoption as a two thousand-year-old history of a major religion that began with the death of its prophet, Jesus Christ. As the centuries passed, it strengthened its hold by altering historical accounts to suit its own agenda and remorselessly subsuming other beliefs into its central core of doctrine and many of these alternative beliefs were entirely magickal in nature.

From the books of the Old Testament to the narratives of the New Testament, it is littered with spectacular displays of magickal events, all of which have gained acceptance as either miracles or the acts of a magickal

Creator God and all based entirely on faith alone. Equally astonishing, from an enlightened point of view, is the assumption that the phenomena described are not regarded as magickal at all, but merely the miraculous acts of a supreme being. The Bible even contains the rituals and incantations required to invoke and solicit the power of the deity it explains and justifies.

The traditional grimoires are packed full of magickal information and they too function in a similar, faith-based manner, so in that way, at least, they are similar to the unthinking observance required by those who believe in religions.

If judged by that yardstick, might the Torah and the Qur'an, with their prayers and incantations, also be adjudged as grimoires? The answer to that question is yes, they can, because both of these systems of worship also have magickal attributes and overtones.

However, all of them are considerably less honest, to the point of embarrassment, about this. If they could open themselves up to closer inspection about the driving force behind them, then it would take away the terrible yoke of fear, compulsion and guilt that hangs like a dark cloak over their adherents. If they could do this and allow some light (and truth) in, their followers might awaken from the slumber that blinds them to the reality of what awaits.

It is the same for you, for you are the key and making this happen lies within your gift. All you have to do is turn it and discover what lies on the other side. If you can do this, prepare to be delighted, for in the truth there is a whole new, liberating universe.

Some Words of Power

The following list of so-called 'Words of Power' is by no mean exhaustive and, in many cases, words are used that have no meaning whatsoever and are entirely made-up on the spur of the moment. By and large, though, the many names of God and/or Christ are considered to be 'natural' words of power, which is why they often appear in grimoires. According to biblical tradition, it was the secret name of God that created the universe, hence its immense potential for good or evil. This mirrors exactly what we saw about the use of magick. The considerable power of the magickal process has no inherent ethics or morality - that comes entirely from whoever wields it.

Alpha, Agla, Cados, Ea, El, Elohim, Eloa, Sabaoth, Shaddi, Adonai, Ehyeh, Jehovah, Yah, Yhvh, Adny, Hain, Lon, Hilay, Radisha, Messias, Emmanuel, Ischyros, Tetragrammaton, Shemhamforash, Omega

Of course the many names of Satan and his lieutenants are used as well for exactly the same reason. But, as far as magicians are concerned, and chaos magicians in particular, whatever works is sufficient and this is reflected in how they operate. As a matter of interest, Satan also has a 'real name', which, appropriately, is the name of God, spelled backwards. One version records this as 'Havayoth'. The idea that anything evil must be the reverse of what is considered good also finds expression in Satanists and black magicians saying the Lord's Prayer backwards, which is used during their conjurations. One of the above mentioned grimoires, the Grimorium Verum advises the sorcerer to have the words, Yod He Vau He, Metatron, Yod, Cados, Eloym and Sabaoth (all words of power, with 'Metatron', according to Jewish rabbinical lore, being the name of an angel) engraved around his inkwell to ward off evil influences. Perhaps this suggestion should also be applied, in some manner, to word processing equipment when it is being used to record material such as this or, perhaps, the very act of typing in the words automatically protects the equipment. It is an interesting, if speculative, thought.

Magickal Numbers

We already saw that the Pythagoreans considered that numbers, because of their sheer ubiquity in relation to the spiritual, natural and scientific worlds, could describe everything and, therefore, contained considerable magickal power. Here is a brief example of why.

The followers of Pythagoras considered that the fundamental numbers for the entire universe were one to ten, since all else was composed of varying combinations of these numbers. One equalled unity and, therefore, God. Two equalled duality and, therefore, Satan (a very early nod towards gnosticism). Four was regarded as sacred and was used when they swore solemn oaths and was probably originator of the expression to 'stand foursquare'. There are also four elements, four seasons, four cardinal points on the compass and four evangelists, all of which may also be linked to the Pythagoreans and their beliefs. Five was their number by which they solemnised marriage. The magician, Cornelius Agrippa, also believed in the power of numbers for reasons similar to those of the Pythagoreans, but Agrippa goes on to point out that the number five, as it appears in nature (he uses the herb, cinquefoil, as an example), can be used to drive out demons, provide relief from fevers and act as an antidote to poison. The links to the magickal attributes of the five-pointed pentagram are unmistakable (the Seal of Solomon again).

In the case of the ancient divinatory art of gematria, where numbers are used in the place of letters, this can happen. Here, the translation key is the simplest and most natural system of alphabetic numeration possible: i.e. the substitution of a letter by its position in the alphabet. So, for English words, A = 1, B = 2, C = 3... Z = 26.

An example of English gematria based on this system (which works well using other languages and was originally devised in Greek and Hebrew) reveals that:

> Jesus Christ = 151
> Holy Spirit = 151
> Jesus is Lord = 151
> Lord of Hosts = 151
> Christ the King = 151
> The Sacrificial Lamb = 151

From this, it appears that the number, 151, has the potential for use as a number of power. The same is true of the number 12 since 1+2 =3, a number cognate with the Holy Trinity of Father, Son and Holy Spirit. In addition to this, 12 was the number of letters in one of the names of God, as were the numbers 42 and 72. This connection may help explain the fascination with the number 12 in other areas, such as the fact that:

> There are 12 Sephiroth on the Tree of Life
> There are 12 tribes of Judah
> Jesus was born at midnight, 12 PM
> Jesus preached in the temple aged 12
> Jesus had 12 apostles
> Adonis, Osiris, and Mithras also had 12 disciples, which is appropriate considering their position as the alleged forerunners of Christ
> There are 12 months in the year
> There are 24 hours (12+12) in the day
> King Arthur had 12 Knights of the Round Table
> Shia Islam has 12 Imams
> The Hindu sun god, Surva, has 12 names
> The Chinese use a 12-year time cycle
> There are 12 houses in the Zodiac

There are many, many more examples of numbers that have achieved unusual prominence in everyday use with no thought to their magickal origins. 7 is a case in point, although this may well stem from something as basic as the fact that there are 7 days in the week. There is also the immense, magickal significance associated with being either a seventh son or, better yet, the seventh son of a seventh son. Something as simple as the prominence and unconscious significance of certain numbers in our lives stems from the world around us and, of course, from the cosmos itself and, once again, we find a reflection of the fundamental and overriding gnostic truism 'as above so below'.

As a final word on the possible significance of numbers, note that when the digits in the previously mentioned number, 151, are added together, the total is 7. Whether or not this actually means anything is open to debate, but it is yet one more bizarre synchronicity in the endlessly fascinating enigma of the magickal universe.

Sources and References

I can thoroughly endorse and recommend all of these works to anyone who desires to expand their knowledge of occult matters. Each one is packed full of valuable information and, most importantly, they are extremely accessible and do not confuse matters by using jargon or archaic phrasing. Admittedly, a few of them may not be available through your local library or particularly easy to track down, if you wish to buy a copy (which I suggest you consider), but Amazon is an excellent source of second-hand material.

An Encyclopaedia of Occultism by Lewis Spence, published in 1996 by Citadel Press, ISBN 0-8065-1401-9.

Note This remarkable book was first published in 1920 and this is its most recent reprint. I can thoroughly recommend it as an absolute goldmine of hard-to-find magickal, occult and esoteric information. In truth, one could almost categorise it among the list of grimoires.

The Golden Bough by Sir James Frazer, published in 1993 by Wordsworth Editions, ISBN 1-85326-310-9

Demons by Anthony Findlay, published in 1989 by Blandford, ISBN 0-7137-2720-9

The Magical Arts by Richard Cavendish, published in 1984 by Arkana, ISBN 0-14-019152-6

The Occult Conspiracy by Michael Howard, published in 1989 by Destiny Books, ISBN 0-89281-251-6

Supernatural by Graham Hancock, published in 2005 by Arrow Books, ISBN 9780099947419

The Book of English Magic by Philip Carr-Gomm & Richard Heygate, published in 2009 by John Murray, ISBN 978-1-84854-041-5

The Secret History of Lucifer by Lynn Picknet, published in 2005 by Robinson, ISBN 10:1-84529-263-4

Lucifer Rising by Gavin Baddely, published in 1999 by Plexus, ISBN 0-85965-280-7

The Occult by Colin Wilson, published in 1979 by Panther Books, ISBN 0-586-05050-7

Secret Wisdom by Ruth Clydesdale, published in 2009 by Arcturus Publishing, ISBN -978-1-84837-241-2

An Exorcist Tells His Story by Fr Gabriele Amorth, published in 1999 by Ignatius Press, ISBN 0898707102

American Exorcism by Michael W. Cluneo, published in 2002 by Bantam Books, ISBN 0-553-81419-2

The Field by Lynn McTaggart, published in 2001 by Element, ISBN 0-00-714510-1

The Directory of Possibilities edited by Colin Wilson & John Grant, published in 1982 by Corgi, ISBN 0-552-11994-6

The Hole in The Sky by Brian Allan, published in 2005 by TGS Hidden Mysteries

Rosslyn, Between Two Worlds by Brian Allan, published by TGS Hidden Mysteries

The Head of God by Keith Laumer, published in 1998 by Weidenfeld & Nicholson, ISBN 0-297-84129-7

In the Name of The Gods by David Elkington, published in 2000 by Green Man Press, ISBN 978-0953993000

Websites Visited

For additional information for the reader, I have added a few comments to this list of websites, where appropriate, and, before reading, please bear in mind that the creators of some of these sites have their own agenda and it is not necessarily helpful, but some of the nuggets of information gained were fascinating. In general, though, the information derived from Wikipedia sources can be regarded as accurate, although, due to its structure, it is also open to abuses, but those who run and police it try to remove unwanted, biased and inaccurate additions as quickly as possible.

en.wikipedia.org/wiki/Affair_of_the_Poisons

en.wikipedia.org/wiki/Joseph-Antoine_Boullan

www.perillos.com/bs_secretsocieties2.html

en.wikipedia.org/wiki/Montespan

www.themystica.com/mystica/articles/s/satanism_history_of.html

en.wikipedia.org/wiki/Black_Mass

www.satansheaven.com/black_mass.htm

www.unicorngarden.com/vamp01.htm

sacred-texts.com/goth/vkk/index.htm

en.wikipedia.org/wiki/Montague_Summers

www.catholicwarfare.com/

Websites such as this should be read while keeping in mind that the Catholic Church has a considerable reputation to defend and has openly declared that it is the only true version of the Christian or, indeed, any faith.

en.wikipedia.org/wiki/Gabriele_Amorth

www.weirdload.com/martin.html

sabbathrock.com/evil.aspx

The information is interesting, but extremely polarised.

http://www.jesus-is-savior.com/False Religions/RomanCatholicism/
satanism_in_the_vatican.htm

Be wary of what is written here. Much of it is written from an Evangelical, Protestant Pentecostalist viewpoint.

www.weirdload.com/martin.html

Once again, this is highly polarised, because the various claims made over the years by former priest and author, Fr Malachi Martin, are, to say the least, contentious. In one sense, it is possible to regard him as a genuine and well-motivated exorcist and demonologist and, in another, as a sensation-seeking scandalmonger.

www.controverscial.com/Aleister%20Crowley.htm

en.wikipedia.org/wiki/Aleister_Crowley

Regarding the relevance of Crowley to the canon of occult and magickal knowledge currently existing today, next to obtaining one of the many, first class biographies written about the mage, this entry on Wikipedia is as good as you are likely to find, the plus side being that there is no readily apparent hidden agenda either pro or con.

www.religioustolerance.org › History › Gnosticism

en.wikipedia.org/wiki/Gnosticism

www.christian-history.org/gnostic-beliefs.html

en.wikipedia.org/wiki/Magic_and_religion

www.chaosmatrix.org/library/chaos/texts/intchaos.html

grimoires.avalonia.co.uk/magic/list.htm

The information on this site is gleaned from the excellent research on the chronology of grimoires conducted by David Rankine.

warlockasylum.wordpress.com/2009/04/23/warlock-asylums-top-20-list-of-grimoires-and-occult-works/

Ritualmagick.co.uk

This particular site is the home page of David Rankine and is well worth a visit from anyone interested in Wicca or, indeed, any other form of magick.

en.wikipedia.org/wiki/Petit_Albert

en.wikipedia.org/wiki/Testament_of_Solomon

www.esotericarchives.com/solomon/testamen.htm

www.renaissanceastrology.com/picatrix.html

www.aztlan.net/bush_vs_kerry.htm

en.wikipedia.org/wiki/Malachi_Martin

www.weirdload.com/martin.html

11th Dimension Publishing

More books from 11th Dimension Publishing!

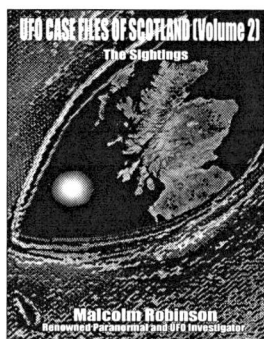

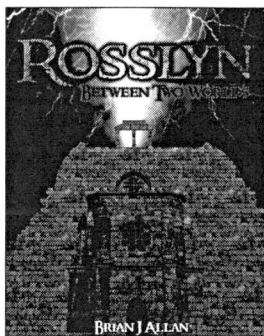

Lightning Source UK Ltd.
Milton Keynes UK
UKOW04f0015290414

230759UK00016BB/781/P